CASES IN HOLISTIC MISSION

By
Word,
Work
and
Wonder

Thomas H. McAlpine

**MARC**

A division of World Vision International
121 E. Huntington Drive, Monrovia, California 91016-3400 USA

By Word, Work and Wonder

Thomas H. McAlpine

ISBN 0-912552-92-1

Published by MARC, a division of World Vision International, 121 East Huntington Drive, Monrovia, California 91016-3400, U.S.A.

Printed in the United States of America. Editor and page layout: Edna G. Valdez. Cover design: Steven J. Singley.

Contents

Acknowledgements

It is a pleasure to acknowledge two networks that have contributed to this book.

The first is the World Vision Partnership. Through this network I learned of the ministries described in chapters 2-5 of this book. World Vision national offices often facilitated visits, and their responses to my early drafts strengthened my material. For the opportunity to work with these colleagues I am deeply grateful.

The second network is the journal *Transformation: An International Dialogue on Evangelical Social Ethics*. Edited by Tokunboh Adeyemo, Vinay Samuel and Ronald Sider, it was initially associated with the Unit of Ethics and Society of the World Evangelical Fellowship Theological Commission, and has subsequently found a home in the Oxford Centre for Mission Studies. Beginning with its April/June 1985 issue, *Transformation* began offering the series of articles, "Wholistic models of evangelism and social concern," whose concerns ran parallel to those of this book. Material that appears in this book first appeared in that series of articles. I have learned from both the journal and from the series, and have included the bulk of the series in my analysis. I believe that *Transformation* continues to exemplify what is best in the evangelical movement.

1

The Context

I am among those rediscovering that God's salvation is holistic. One of the statements coming out of Lausanne '74 expresses this rediscovery well:

> The *evangel* is God's Good News in Jesus Christ; it is Good News of the reign he proclaimed and embodies; of God's mission of love to restore the world to wholeness through the Cross of Christ and him alone; of his victory over the demonic powers of destruction and death; of his Lordship over the entire universe; it is Good News of a new creation of a new humanity, a new birth through him by his life-giving Spirit; of the gifts of the messianic reign contained in Jesus and mediated through him by his Spirit; of the charismatic community empowered to embody his reign of shalom here and now before the whole creation and make his Good News seen and known. It is Good News of liberation, of restoration, of wholeness, and of salvation that is personal, social, global and cosmic. Jesus is Lord! Alleluia! Let the earth hear his voice!

I continue to ask what this holism means for mission practice. This is not an easy task, because mission practitioners and thinkers have varied understandings of holistic mission, and even the language we use can get in the way.

This book does not assume that there is a single ideal expression of holism. Context and tradition foster diversity. So we need a variety of stories to push our thinking and acting.

I do need to indicate what I believe holistic mission involves. My provisional answer, which affected the selection of the ministries I describe in this book, is the following statement:

> *The Christian community is to be a sign of the kingdom, in which evangelism, social action and the Spirit are present and inseparably related.*

"The Christian community is to be a sign of the kingdom . . ."

Discussions of "holism" often start by asking if evangelism and social action are present, and how they connect. There is a prior question, however, stressed recently by Lesslie Newbigin.

> The central reality is neither word nor act, but the total life of a community enabled by the Spirit to live in Christ, sharing his passion and the power of his resurrection. (1989, 137)

This encourages us to begin with the life of the community, which is the base for its various ministries.

". . . in which evangelism, social action and the Spirit are present and inseparably related"

For "evangelism," I like William Abraham's definition: "That set of intentional activities which is governed by the goal of initiating people into the kingdom of God for the first time." (1989, 95)

I understand social action as *that set of intentional activities governed by the goal of the community becoming a God-fearing agent of its own history.* These activities range from relief to development to structural change. "Community" here refers to the larger community in which the local church or churches are located.

The reference to the Holy Spirit reflects the experience of a growing number of communities in ministry, only some of whom identify with Pentecostal or charismatic groups. The issue is not primarily particular "gifts of the Spirit," but the broader question of where and how we expect the Spirit to act, and of what actions we seek. Thus, by "Spirit" I mean *the Spirit of Christ acting to empower individuals and communities for personal and social change.* The point of saying "the Spirit of *Christ*" is to remind us that we have not stopped talking about the kingdom of God.

Obviously, my concerns are not neutral. The danger is that I will use them in a heavy-handed way, a straitjacket in which the ministry is invited to dance. That is not my intent. I will let the ministry define its own terms. Only at the end will I raise questions about how the ministry speaks to the concerns with which I began.

The expressions of ministry surveyed in this book will all have their own strengths and weaknesses. When set side by side, my hope is that these expressions will assist us in our work.

Thus, "What is holistic mission?" is the deceptively simple question this book seeks to address. The question is deceptively simple because we can understand it either descriptively (what does holistic mission look like in practice?) or normatively (what should holistic mission look like?). Again, deceptively simple because it leaves unidentified the context in which the question arises. The remainder of this chapter addresses these issues.

A. The Context

I write from within World Vision, a Christian development and relief organization, which characteristically interprets its work to churches as an exercise in holistic mission. World Vision's charism is more action than reflection, and so our reflection on holistic mission is largely done on the run. (This manuscript itself reflects that pattern: the studies were done between November 1991 and December 1993, with the editing completed while I was on secondment to World Vision's office in Costa Rica in 1994-95.)

World Vision, in turn, draws its understanding of holistic mission both from its own practice and from the larger Christian and development communities, primarily from that evangelical sector represented by the Lausanne Committee for World Evangelization (LCWE) and journals such as *Transformation* or *Urban Mission*. To identify the context for this book, I will review that larger conversation by following C. René Padilla, who picks up that conversation in 1966. A more comprehensive review of the conversation in the United States would need to look at the holistic mission of the nineteenth century and the subsequent evangelical retreat to the evangelization of individuals (see Dayton 1976, Marsden 1980).

Padilla (1985) describes the evangelical pilgrimage from 1966 to 1983, and in so doing shows us examples of the implicit definition of holism as evangelism plus social responsibility (word and work). To illustrate this latter point, at the beginning of the survey Padilla states:

> A number of . . . conferences . . . reflect this debate [the relationship between evangelism and social responsibility]. A gleaning of the documents that emerged from them . . . shows that a more wholistic approach to mission has slowly gained ground in evangelical circles.

At the end of the survey we find:

> The "marriage" between evangelism and social responsibility as a wholistic approach to mission was confirmed . . .

4

While "holism" is a term Padilla finds useful, it is not a term highlighted in the documents themselves. I note this to clarify that the purpose of this book is not to enshrine "holism" in our vocabulary, but to ask what we have been learning about its use. Other words (e.g., the reign of God, *shalom*) can be used to point in the same direction, and in some contexts may be more useful.

In 1966 the Wheaton Declaration, product of the Congress on the Church's Worldwide Mission, articulated the desire to "look to the Scriptures for guidance as to expressing social concern, without minimizing the priority of preaching the Gospel of individual salvation." Social concern has a place on the mission agenda, albeit a somewhat tenuous one, and it is emphatically subordinated to the evangelization of individuals. In 1974 the Lausanne Covenant, product of the International Congress on World Evangelization, recognized that "evangelism and socio-political involvement are both parts of our Christian duty." Padilla writes—too optimistically—"The Lausanne Covenant was a death blow to every attempt to reduce the mission of the Church to the multiplication of Christians and churches through evangelism" (1985, 29).

But what is the relationship between evangelism and sociopolitical involvement? The Theology and Education Group of the LCWE and the Unit on Ethics and Society of the Theological Commission of the World Evangelical Fellowship co-sponsored the Consultation on the Relationship between Evangelism and Social Responsibility (CRESR) in 1982 to deal with this issue. Evangelism and sociopolitical involvement, declared the report, "while distinct from one another, are integrally related in our proclamation of and obedience to the Gospel. The partnership is, in reality, a marriage" (CRESR 1982, 24). Again, Padilla: "In contrast with all the previous documents produced by evangelicals in the last few years, it clarified that the primacy of evangelism can only be stated in a relative, not in an absolute, sense" (1983, 29).

How does this relationship work out in practice? CRESR identified three types of relations:

- ❖ First, social activity is a *consequence* of evangelism.
- ❖ Second, social activity can be a *bridge* to evangelism.
- ❖ Third, social activity not only follows evangelism as its consequence and aim, and precedes it as its bridge, but also accompanies it as its *partner*. (1982, 21-23)

Padilla's review makes it clear that progress in the acceptance and implementation of CRESR's understanding of holism as word and work was neither steady nor unproblematic.

Another contribution to the evangelical discussion, that of the shift from holism as word-work to holism as word-work-wonder, was the Pentecostal/Charismatic and Evangelical Social Activist Conference in Sierra Madre, California in January 1988. The David DuPlessis Center for Christian Spirituality at Fuller Theological Seminary was host to the conference. Michael Harper, international executive director of SOMA (an Anglican charismatic renewal organization), and Ronald Sider (executive director of Evangelicals for Social Action) coordinated the gathering.

The papers and findings report of the conference appeared in *Transformation* 5/4 (October/December 1988). Two paragraphs from that report provide key summaries of the discussion that took place.

> Increasingly, an emphasis upon the kingdom of God has become central in the theology of both evangelical social activists and Pentecostals/charismatics. The former, however, have tended to emphasize the relationship of the kingdom to justice for the poor, and the latter have tended to stress the importance of spiritual gifts, spiritual power, and signs and wonders. As we looked again at the Scriptures together, we saw more clearly that both concerns are central to the biblical teaching on the kingdom

of God. Only as we grasp and apply the total Good News of the kingdom is the full evangelistic power of the Gospel released. Words, works, and wonders belong together as we seek to live faithfully a biblical theology of the kingdom of God.

In theological discussion and reflection on practical models we felt drawn powerfully to a common vision for a kingdom community where we all live under the cross, rejoicing in the Saviour's unmerited forgiveness and knowing him as our life; where personal righteousness, work for justice, peace, and freedom are all grounded in Spirit-guided worship and prayer; where the Bible's special concern for the poor finds powerful expression; where signs and wonders bestowed by the Holy Spirit direct and empower a holistic witness that draws multitudes to repentance and faith in the Lord of the kingdom. (1988, 1-2)

As the last clause of the quotation shows, "holistic" has been used—as it is used in this book—to point to the desired result of this conversation, this search.

"Holistic," then, as it is described here, signals a search to minister more adequately. "More adequately" refers primarily to specific situations of ministry. The studies that follow reflect this response to specific situations. "Our efforts to evangelize and disciple this group kept running up against their homelessness," reports a member of Ichthus in London. "We had to address that. Our ministry had to become more holistic." But "more adequately" can also refer to other concerns: for example, to create space for those bringing gifts different from ours to ministry, or to create space for a re-encounter with a particular grace of God.

B. This Study

In the context of the foregoing summary, my challenge was to identify and describe groups (church or parachurch)

7

involved in holistic mission. What does holistic mission look like in practice?

I relied on various networks to help me put together several itineraries and I traveled. I had the opportunity to visit more ministries than I describe here, sharing their dreams, sharing meals, having my own faith and vision renewed and challenged. The results of four of these visits appear in this book as the studies in chapters 2-5.

At roughly the same time, the journal *Transformation* published a series on "Wholistic models of evangelism and social concern," trying to get—broadly speaking—at the same question. There has been some overlap in our efforts. Roger Forster's description of Ichthus Christian Fellowship—a group I also had the privilege of visiting and describing—appears in the *Transformation* series. My description of the Parish of the Resurrection in Mexico City was also included in the *Transformation* series.

Obviously, not my descriptions, but the life and ministry of these churches and parachurch groups are the important things. Each uniquely seeks to live out what it means to be the church universal in a particular setting. Trying to simply duplicate any of their ministries without attending to the particular context would be a major mistake.

Nevertheless, it is worth asking what we can learn from them. That was the initial point of my travels—to get a clearer idea as to what this "holism" was about. Each study in this book contains an initial attempt to define and describe it.

As a result, included here are my studies of Ichthus Christian Fellowship (London), the Nazarene Center in San Mateo (Colombia) and the Parish of the Resurrection in Mexico City. In addition, I also studied the methodology of Scripture Search in the projects of World Vision in the Philippines.

Why did I include Scripture Search? I return to the findings report from the Sierra Madre conference: "We shared a common commitment to the Bible as our authority and inspiration and to the Holy Spirit as our guide, convictor, and empowerer" (1988, 1). Scripture must inform all practice of and reflection on holistic mission. Nevertheless, we can assume neither our ability to hear Scripture nor the appropriateness of the ways we approach Scripture. Consequently, the experience of Scripture Search, in which there is a fit between the practice of holistic mission and the conversation with Scripture, is an important contribution to my reflection on holistic mission.

Following the four studies, I summarize the first fourteen *Transformation* studies. I refer to these studies in the analysis; the point of the summaries is to provide at least some context for these references.

Following these summaries, I offer an analysis in two stages. First, what dimensions of holism stand out? This is a preliminary and impressionistic review of the set. Second, what is the emerging profile of holism? This part is more prescriptive, as it attempts to identify dimensions of holism that are worth encouraging.

Does this imply that the question "What is holistic mission?" is a descriptive or normative question? Certainly, the process of selecting the ministries involves both implicit and explicit criteria. The final chapter does advocate broadening our concept of the term "holistic." Nevertheless, the point of this book is the ministries: "Go and tell John what you hear and see . . ." (Matt. 11:4). And the point of the question, "What is holistic mission?" is that in an increasing number of places this invitation of Jesus will be repeated. "Go and tell John what you hear and see in Madras, in Moscow, in Mozambique."

2

Ichthus
Christian Fellowship

In 1974 the Evangelical Alliance (the primary grouping of evangelical church and parachurch entities in the United Kingdom) sponsored the "Power Project" to encourage local evangelism across the United Kingdom. In Forest Hill, a community in southeast London, Roger and Faith Forster, Roger and Sue Mitchell and others keen on evangelism came together and, at the project's end, wished to continue their work. Their particular concern was for the large government housing estates, which had proven to be the grave of many evangelistic efforts. Local churches gave their blessing to this vision, and Ichthus Christian Fellowship was born with 14 adults plus children, ranging from a newborn to two women past their sixties.

Why "Ichthus"? Roger Forster explains the name: "It is, of course, an acrostic for 'Jesus Christ, Son of God, Saviour', and was used as a sign . . . by the early church. . . . Because we wished to be radical in the sense of going back to our New Testament roots, and so charming away centuries of religious accretions, we preferred the fish as our symbol before any other.

Added to this we wanted fish for Jesus: 'Come after me and I will make you fishers of men' (Mark 1:17). We are only interested in conversion growth, not transfers. Also, Jesus ate fish at his resurrection (Luke 24:42-43) to show it was a 'real' resurrection. We believe he really is active—tangibly alive, and is interested in our tangible, real human existence."[1]

All three parts of Forster's response are important. First, Ichthus attempts to bring Scripture and late twentieth century England into direct conversation with each other. What of the intervening 20 centuries of church history? In early 1992 Forster wrote a series in *Celebration* (Ichthus' monthly magazine) titled "Roots and Shoots" with articles like "Waldensians, Albigensians, and St. Francis." Second, "fishers of men" underscores the concern for evangelism, which in Ichthus is the covering term for all of its mission. Third, the emphasis on Jesus being tangibly alive in human existence underscores a robust faith in the power of the gospel to transform life here and now. As Roger Mitchell says, "The work of the Kingdom is not so much to get people out of earth into heaven, but to get as much heaven as possible on to this earth and into people."

Today, over 20 years later, there are 28 Ichthus congregations: 21 are in southeast London, three in north London, two in southwest London, and two in Kent. These congregations comprise about 1,600 adults and several hundred children in Sunday morning congregational meetings. In addition, there are another five communities in the Middle East and in France.

The phrase "the kingdom" is used a great deal within Ichthus. An important strength of Ichthus is the way in which this vision of the kingdom has shaped daily life. "The kingdom" is understood in terms of three principles that have been important from the start: love, humility and openness to the Holy Spirit. Forster recalls, "We simply made a commitment to love one another and to build relationships of trust and forgiveness." Experience in other congregations had impressed on them the

need "to avoid being critical or unpleasant about each other."
Humility, reflects Forster, was demanded by their context: "The
sheer complexity of life and humanity means that we are con-
stantly faced with problems to which only the fresh wisdom of
the Holy Spirit can give us the answer." What does this mean
in practice? "Authoritarian structures were avoided and authoritarian means of organising church life were disliked. Humility
extended to accepting other churches and groups as having
their own validity." Openness to the Holy Spirit was expressed
in a variety of ways within Ichthus. It assumed new importance
in 1982 when the Forsters' son came down with a leukaemic
type of cancer. There was a massive outpouring of prayer and
when someone from the United States with the gift of healing
ministered powerfully, their son was healed. "We all discovered
the power of prayer," Forster recounts, "the meaning of love and
commitment and the importance of unity." This experience
secured within Ichthus a major place for the charismatic
dimension.

But what have love, humility and openness to the Holy
Spirit meant concerning questions of race and male-female
roles? When it came to leadership, the decision was made early:
the issue was gifting, not gender or ethnicity.

A commitment to a particular pattern of ministry has
been important from the start: fellowship, mission and training.
Regarding fellowship, Forster said: "We determined to commit
ourselves to one another and share our lives as fully as we
could. Any success we may have had in our history has grown
out of the fellowship of love and commitment to one another.
To laugh and cry together, to be loyal in word and deed: these
are still basic to our church life." Mission is understood to
embrace evangelism, social action and foreign missions. Ichthus
members work as tentmakers in many countries, and their stories are prominent in the Ichthus journal *Celebration*. Training
is always on-the-job, and extensive. "Roger Forster's intention,"

says one of his associates, "is to spoil people from doing anything else with their lives."

This intentional combination of fellowship, training, and mission powerfully shapes both the culture of Ichthus (including its "feel") and its viability. And as the following sketches of congregations illustrate, the combination is reproduced on the congregational level.

Three Congregations

What does Ichthus look like? What follows are descriptions of three congregations: City Gates (Soho), North Peckham and the Brown Bear (Deptford).

City Gates

Ichthus' City Gates congregation is located in Soho, home to London's theaters, youth-oriented shops and the red-light district. The location is not accidental. A congregational leader recalls: "I felt a strong desire to see God's work being carried out in the very center of London"; and so a group from Ichthus worked with a Youth With A Mission team to form a congregation in the middle of Soho.

This decision put them at the beginning of a new learning curve, as they sought to minister to the needs of the people in this area. They started meetings in Leicester Square (a popular gathering point for youth) with lunch afterward, which tended to attract the homeless. As they began to disciple new contacts, they discovered that it was hard to disciple people who have no address. So they began to deal with the issue of homelessness. In another situation, one new Christian decided that his conversion also meant confessing at the police station. The police did not believe him—until he wrote a detailed confession. The City Gates church leader spoke on his behalf: we'll vouch for him and take care of him. This led to the opening of Ichthus's first rehabilitation house with this youth and two others.

In working with the homeless, City Gates has used outreach teams with weekly visits to the area where youth sleep out to make contact, to provide support and friendship, to build trust (trust is characteristically a rare commodity in this context). The teams provide food, clothing and sleeping bags. They have opened a hospitality center or coffee bar. The coffee bar is a place for counseling, advice and hostel referral; it offers food, tea, coffee, a welcome shower and clothing. City Gates has also opened a first-stage rehab house with a full-time rehabilitation program; congregation members there provide counseling and deal with various addictions, prostitution and homosexuality. Deliverance and emotional healing also play important roles.

Subsequently, City Gates has shifted from a major focus on the homeless to concentrating on a number of people groups as foci for cell group ministry: red-light area workers, students in universities and the international community (there are 15 to 20 different nationalities in the church). Resources formally put into the homeless ministry are now available via the cell groups and personal relationships. The approach is more that of an extended family, less that of a social action approach of food distribution. Says one leader: "We wanted something closer to the extended family: come and live in my home. Be part of us in who we are."

The work with prostitutes has turned out to be highly time-intensive and is increasingly the responsibility of a number of people who have devoted full-time ministry here. Nevertheless, there is also a canvassing of the area during major holidays when members of the congregation give gifts (pots of jam, personalized cards) and—at Christmas—sing Christmas carols. On at least one occasion the carolers were invited to sing onstage at one of the local strip clubs.

Of the 60-70 members in the congregation, 10-15 have become Christians through City Gates' ministry. For many in the congregation who have Christian backgrounds, City Gates has been a place to mature and deepen commitments. Others are like the woman from a well-established suburban church that did not believe in women in leadership. Here people get pushed into leadership positions that stretch them in many ways.

The normal approach to a place like Soho would be through specialized ministry teams. While Ichthus has done this where there was no other option (e.g., the slow relationship-building being done by a woman working with prostitutes), it prefers that the congregation itself do the ministering. Thus of the 60-70 people who form the City Gates congregation, 40-50 work in the coffee bar and 8 more make up the outreach teams. To be part of the church is to be part of the church's outreach. To put the last point differently, Ichthus differs from the usual pattern in which people first decide to join a church and subsequently decide to involve themselves in that church's ministry. Here, joining the congregation means becoming part of the ministry team.

One leader observes: "Homelessness is not simply a question of having a roof over your head. We have to deal with root causes, and give people family, security, and so on. We have to deal with the root issues." There is a link between this insight and the congregation-based ministry. To perceive of homelessness as simply a technical matter means that a technical solution implemented by technical folk is appropriate. Since the problem is seen as interwoven with a whole set of issues, it is the congregation itself that provides the appropriate context and agent for dealing with these.

Where do the members expect or seek the Holy Spirit's work? The Spirit's work is characteristically implicit rather than explicit, whether in the love of the community, inner healing, deep therapy or deliverance. Where there is success in the rehabilitation house, it is the Spirit's work, whatever the particular means. The congregation has also been learning that the

15

Spirit works in different ways in response to different sorts of needs, so that the congregation's ministry needs more variety. They are, for instance, moving away from the strategy of seeking to pray everyone off drugs (as in the model they had previously adopted). And now they do not call their evangelism "friendship evangelism" but "prayer evangelism," since its basis is prayer for people by name.

North Peckham Estates

This area is a group of public housing projects characterized by high crime, unemployment and single-parent families. About 80 percent of the residents are behind in their rent payments, and the average amount in arrears is £1,000 (approximately US$2,000). Neglect and abuse of children is prevalent.

Here the Ichthus congregation meets in the Wells Way Baptist Church. The congregation is nine years old. There are currently 120 adults and 35 children; about 30 percent of the adults have become Christians through this ministry.

In the congregation, the neighborhood context illustrates that becoming a Christian means a long process of lifestyle changes, particularly in the areas of parenting patterns, substance abuse, gambling and debt. Key to the congregation's social action is a conviction that Jesus desires the kingdom to come, and a wealth of people prepared to work for low wages. Specialized ministries include two nursery schools and a primary school, an employment training program and, until recently, a launderette-coffee shop.

The launderette-coffee shop occupied a large welcomingly-lit room on the ground floor of one of the estates. Getting there meant walking past graffiti-covered walls and large mongrels of dubious temper. Inside was a warm welcome, a clean place to do laundry with machines that worked, a place for the kids to play and a table for tea and sweets with a friend in between attending to the machines. One woman who became a Christian in this setting brought some of the warmth back to her home. Her husband became a Christian too, which for him meant doing something about his rack of knives—each carrying the name of an intended victim. But due to repeated break-ins on the premises, the launderette-coffee shop is currently closed.

The schools are a response to the undervaluing of children and family in the estates. Staff see themselves as engaged in "spiritual warfare: love and service cut against the spirit of the age, and begin to break barriers." One expression of this commitment to love and service is that the staff pray regularly for the children and their families. (It is worth noticing that the more usual pattern in the house church movement in the United Kingdom is to start schools for their own membership. These Ichthus schools are part of seeking the *shalom* of all of North Peckham.)

Of bringing their child to the school, one parent said: "This is the most significant thing I've done in my life." In another case, the staff prayed for a mother who was neglecting her daughter. The next week the mother came by: "I want to change my mind about my daughter. Can you teach me how to make my daughter happy at home too?"

PECAN[2] (the Peckham Evangelical Churches Action Network) runs—among other things—employment preparation courses. The staff fill these courses through intense recruiting (10,000 households were personally contacted an average of three times each in 1990-1991). The course starts with a one-day workshop, designed to whet the appetite, which touches on everything from job advertisements (looking at what they say) and job resumes (what they are and how to use them) to mock interviews with feedback provided. After this day-long workshop, students who decide they want more take a four-week course. PECAN's courses have one of the highest success rates nationally, with over half its students finding jobs or in further training (64 percent at the end of 1993).

The PECAN leadership makes clear their Christian identity and the Christian framework within which they present the employment training. At the same time, they are committed to the program's effectiveness and scrupulously avoid serving it as "bait" for evangelism. North Peckham Estates has not lacked gospel words; what PECAN believes it has lacked is gospel life, and the employment training scheme is one expression of that.

That said, there are some interesting spin-offs. One group of students was sufficiently impressed by their trainer that they asked her to run an inquirers'[3] group. That alone would be encouraging; what was more encouraging was that her supervisor's primary concern was that the inquirers' group not adversely affect the quality of the program.

Brown Bear Congregation

In mid-1989 Ichthus leaders decided that they needed to start working on a specific program for youth aged 15-25. Of the 1,500 participants in Ichthus at that time, only 100 were in the 15-25 age group—about 200 less than expected. In September 1990 Ichthus started the youth work at a former pub, the Brown Bear, with a core of 12 people in the desired age range. At the end of 1993, 40 people were involved in house groups, with a somewhat larger number involved in the Friday congregational meeting.

A number of aggressive decisions have determined the particular shape of this congregation. First, Ichthus decided that the program for "their" youth would be the program for outreach to London's pagan youth culture. The easier decision would have been to develop a youth program for their youth that was "safe" and would serve (in part) to insulate the youth from the "world." But one important effect of this decision was that Ichthus youth clearly had a mission that was theirs, and many rose to the challenge.

Second, Ichthus decided to locate in Deptford; the easier decision would have been to choose a "safe" neighborhood.

Deptford is on the south bank of the Thames, one of the last undeveloped areas in the old docklands. It was the site of munitions factories during World War II and its "feel" is such that some Ichthus members talk of territorial spirits (the only site that elicited this language in our conversations). Deptford streets are marked by a simple survival strategy: I intimidate you before you can intimidate me. And Deptford is very popular with London's highly mobile youth culture.

Third, Ichthus decided to locate in an old pub that had come up for sale. For many Christians "pub" implies "the world"; Ichthus desires to see the kingdom grow in precisely that world.

Fourth, Jeff and Muriel Westlake, a retired couple, moved from Chalfont St. Peter, a comfortable suburb, to Deptford to set up and run Brown Bear. This was despite Jeff Westlake's poor health. *Celebration* mentioned this in its obituary following Jeff's death on November 4, 1991:

> Jeff had been ill for some time with kidney problems, but his death was still a shock. Asked earlier in the year whether he didn't think he ought to give up, his reply was that he hadn't yet finished what God told him to do. He was, say members of the youth team, "A wonderful man, utterly committed. He put his all into it, and in his quiet way he had become a special kind of dad to some of the Deptford kids."

Fifth, the youth take multiple leadership roles. The 15-25 year olds lead, preach, pray and pastor. And, despite a wealth of music within Ichthus, Brown Bear produces its own.

The heart of the work is the creation and nurturing of community. What is that? "When folk are caring for and looking after and confessing sins and trusting one another and enjoying being together and serving other people coming into the community, that's family."

The congregation makes regular prayer walks—times of walking and praying together through Deptford's streets. They pray for people. They pray against the territorial spirits, which are experienced in the atmosphere of violence, intimidation and death.

The Brown Bear Pub provides a focal point for ministry. There are weekly family nights. It is a place of contact for the homeless. And the ministry reapplies PECAN's learnings regarding job and life skills training here. The pub further serves as the site for multiple congregation and house group meetings and activities.

What is the role of the Spirit here? The creation of genuine community, empowering of individuals, "discipleship things" and healing of people's lives.

Training

Training is a major component of Ichthus's vision of ministry. Ichthus has designed and gives courses from their orientation course for new Christians to multi-week projects that provide primary training not only for their leadership, but for others looking for hands-on training as well—from inside and outside the United Kingdom. Three items from their training brochures may convey something of the training's spirit:

The first describes Network, currently the primary training module:

> Network is a one year training course running from January to December for spiritually mature Christians wishing to acquire skills in the areas of leadership and church planting, with the opportunity to emphasize youth, cross-cultural evangelism, church growth or church formation in the inner city. The Programme is modular in form and so in some cases can be spread over a number of years by those continuing in full or part time employment.

The second item:

> **What happens if I fall apart?** All those on training courses will have pastoral care and support from both

team leaders and "One to One" partnerships. These people are pastorally-gifted and are there to support in prayer. Regular meetings with One to Ones are encouraged in order to pray through any issues, e.g., personal relationships, spiritual breakthrough, finance, health, family or for general supportive prayer.

The third item is a recurring quotation from Roger Forster:

> What could be the most dramatic breakthrough in the history of world evangelism demands radically trained disciples. Are you ready for the challenge?

These items communicate well Ichthus's vision for training: not simply to impart information or a set of more-or-less integrated skills, but to create a cadre against whom the gates of hell will not prevail.

Mission

From the start, world evangelism has been an Ichthus priority. On the one hand, world evangelism is a mindset, and the slogan "Think globally, act locally" resonates with much of the local action.

On the other hand, the action does not remain local. Senior leaders give time to mission activities outside London including, currently, support for the DAWN (Disciple a Whole Nation) program. The materials Ichthus develops are made available systematically to congregations outside London. Mission is an integral component of Ichthus's training programs. Ichthus members have helped promote March for Jesus in other countries (particularly in Europe) and are engaged in church planting in restrictive contexts, putting to use what they have learned in multi-ethnic London.

The Model

Word, work and wonder

"The mission of the church," argues Forster, "under the direction and in the power of the Holy Spirit, is to evangelise with words, works and wonders, which embody proclamation, presence, and power evangelism as popularly understood. All three are necessary to each other for a holistic appreciation of the task of mission. It is further understood that the whole mission is for the whole body of believers, not a specialized section of the church." Forster finds this three-fold pattern (visualized in Figure 2.1 on page 23) in texts such as Matthew 4:12-25, Acts 10:34-43 and Romans 15:18-19.

Word, work and wonder are held together in a number of ways:

❖ All are seen as evangelization.

❖ All are seen as the work of the Holy Spirit.

❖ Actions characteristically use a combination: during open-air preaching, there may be prayer offered for the sick. During door-to-door evangelism, there may be an invitation to participate in a life-skills course.

As Forster says: "It would (and should) be virtually impossible to untangle the three strands of this evangelistic cord."

Two examples of the delightful difficulty of untangling the cord:

George, now in his eighties, was an ex-policeman, commando and atheist, confined by illness to a wheelchair. One of our workers visited him regularly. George welcomed the chat and one day said to him, "I guess I had better ask this Jesus into my life." "I guess you had better," our man replied. George prayed, and as he did so got out of his wheelchair, then exclaimed, "Goodness me, what

Figure 2.1: Evangelization by word, work and wonder

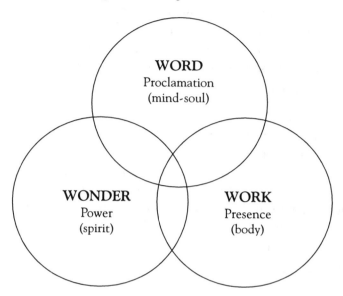

have I done?" He later told us that he had seen a vision of Jesus and had stood up into Jesus' arms and was healed.

On one occasion, when we helped a woman in her nineties who was flooded by a burst pipe, someone knocked on my door and said "Are you the people who dried out Grandmother?" We told her that we were and she said "I want to become a Christian" right on the spot!

Are these stories of word, work or wonder?

Within missiological conversations, Forster has been one of the most articulate advocates of understanding holism in terms of word, work and wonder. The Ichthus Christian Fellowship in general and the congregations described above in particular help us understand what word-work-wonder look like in practice, and how we can make that formulation attractive.

23

Nevertheless, there may be a number of other components in Ichthus that are equally important, and that can contribute to the holism conversation. These components are community, a small group structure, kingdom, the option for the poor and incarnation. I devote the rest of this chapter to exploring them.

Community

"The central reality," suggests Lesslie Newbigin (1989, 137), "is neither word nor act, but the total life of a community enabled by the Spirit to live in Christ, sharing his passion and the power of his resurrection." The community that Ichthus nurtures—present at the start during the commitments of 1974—is the matrix within which word, work and wonder function, first within the community and then outside it in evangelism.

Small group structure

The small-group structure appears to Ichthus to be the social form adequate to express this vision of community. The starting-point is the house or neighborhood group. The larger units (congregation, celebration), as well as the large number of projects underway at any given time (e.g., the life skills courses, the pregnancy counseling unit, the credit bank) exist for these house (neighborhood) groups, and not vice versa.

In this area Ichthus shares similarities with other experiments in decentralizing congregation life, such as the house church movement in the United Kingdom or practitioners such as Ralph Neighbour (*Where Do We Go from Here?—A Guidebook for the Cell Group Church*). But an important difference from many of these experiments is the mission-driven nature of the structure. Ichthus evaluates the structure according to its usefulness for mission—and changes it when necessary.

Kingdom

Kingdom here refers to a shared vision of the kingdom deeply rooting itself in a "patch" (a high-rise apartment building in a housing estate, a neighborhood street and so on). Roger Mitchell (1986, 29-30) articulates this in his book *The Kingdom Factor*:

> A kingdom must have . . . a king, citizens and possessions or lands. . . . In the good news of the kingdom Jesus announces reconciliation with God the king as our father, peace to mankind as our brothers and sisters, and reconciliation with creation as its heirs, its princes and princesses. Put another way, in the gospel, Jesus offers to establish us as a new creation of people, right with God, right with one another and right with everything else. The only condition is that we repent and believe, receive this good news. This is enormous good news which leaves none of reality untouched.

This theme showed up repeatedly in my interviews with Ichthus members: "The gathering of God's people to bring in the kingdom in a place" . . . "You try to discover what relationships are there and try to feed the life of Jesus into the relationships you find there". . . "Get [the] group actively cooperating with the Holy Spirit and creating a community of interdependence."

The option for the poor

"Option for the poor" is not part of Ichthus's vocabulary, but it is a noticeable part of their practice. By the end of 1993, the congregational breakdown was 1/3 inner city, 1/3 transitional zone and 1/3 suburb.

James 2:1-6 has been important in forming Ichthus's ethos. There is a down-to-earth style of spirituality in dress and speech. People arrive at celebrations late, drifting in. Children are welcomed. Someone brings a dog. Congregations meet in community centers and other non-religious buildings. They attempt to keep their language jargon-free. People see the church's commitment to the inner city, and try to join in the mission.

The option is also evident in the way new congregations are formed. The main strategy is to find an area where people have no contact with "living Christianity." Sometimes people ask to start a new congregation in their area (for example, the church in Beckenham—a well-to-do suburb—which did not work). An older woman observed: "If we're to be with the poor, we need to find where the poor are." So the team moved into a local council housing estate, the church grew and additional congregations have subsequently been planted. Ichthus looks to locate its churches one-half to three-quarters miles apart, since most folk do not own cars.

Incarnation

The portrait of the North Peckham Estates congregation suggests two keys to the congregation's social action: a conviction that Jesus desires the kingdom to come, and a wealth of people prepared to work for low wages. Brown Bear became a reality because Jeff and Muriel Westlake moved from suburban retirement into Deptford ministry. And in 1969 Roger and Faith Forster moved to Forest Hill, part of London's twilight zone ("The run-down area you pass through on your way from the more affluent suburbs, like Bromley or Beckenham, to the concrete jungles of really depressed inner city areas like Brixton, Camberwell, Peckham and New Cross" [Forster 1986, 48]). Ichthus does not do ministry at arm's length, and it is costly. But without romanticizing this, it is worth noting that Ichthus folk talk more characteristically about joy than about cost.

Conclusion

Ichthus Christian Fellowship is, as are all the churches described in this book, very much in process. Its importance lies far more in the ways it touches and molds the lives of those in London and (increasingly) beyond than in its contribution to missiological reflection.

That said, its contribution to missiological reflection is not insignificant. It helps us understand what holism conceived as word, work and wonder means in practice. This is not completely accidental, for Roger Forster, senior leader, has also participated in the discussion that has led us to see "word, work and wonder" as a useful working definition. The delightful surprise is how much more is evident at Ichthus than the "word, work and wonder" phrase captures. Community, small-group structure, kingdom, option for the poor and incarnation—these too appear to be part of the dynamic.

NOTES

1   The quoted material in this chapter that does not have accompanying source citations comes from various sources: Roger Forster, "Ichthus Christian Fellowship" in *Ten New Churches* (1986), pp. 48-71; Roger Forster, "Ichthus Christian Fellowship, London" in *Transformation* 5/4 (October/December 1988), pp. 44-46; Roger Mitchell, *The Kingdom Factor: An Introduction to Living in the Kingdom of God* (Marshall Pickering, 1986); and the author's interview with Roger Forster.

2   PECAN (Peckham Evangelical Churches Action Network) is an organization that is independent of Ichthus, but its leadership is largely if not entirely composed of Ichthus leaders.

3   An inquirers' group is a study group for those who would like to learn more about what following Jesus might mean before making a decision regarding whether or not to follow him.

3

Centro Nazareno
San Mateo

The *Centro Nazareno San Mateo* (Nazarene Center of San Mateo) works with the poorest families in Soacha, a city on the outskirts of Bogota, Colombia. The *Centro* has proclaimed the Good News of the kingdom in word, deed and sign since 1988. This proclamation is having a profound effect on Soacha.

Soacha (like Bogota) nestles against the eastern range of the Andes. Vegetation is sparse, the climate cool, the people warm. Soacha has approximately 450,000 inhabitants in about 140 neighborhoods, many of which climb up the sides of the mountains. Sixty percent of these neighborhoods lack public services, schools and health centers. Most of the neighborhoods are the result of "invasions" of squatters associated with various left-wing revolutionary groups. (The area in which the *Centro* is located takes its name from the nearest nonsquatter neighborhood.)

Most of the inhabitants are from the countryside, pulled by the advantages of being near Bogota, pushed by the countryside's endemic violence. The men seek work in the nearby quarries or as day laborers. Too often they lack skills for other jobs, and unemployment is high. To make ends meet, the women must often work out of the home as well. Often, the women raise their families because their husbands have either left home or are drinking their earnings and beating their wives. Children are often at risk, particularly if their parents need to leave them alone during the day.

The *Centro* is working in seven barrios, developing activities in skill training, health, education, housing, family relations, and evangelism. This work flows from the vision of the pastor, Javier Paniagua:

> We stress God's desire that people live in dignity. Dignity is denied in so many ways here. God sees this clearly, and God responds: "'I have seen the affliction of my people who are in Egypt, and have heard their cry because of their taskmasters; I know their sufferings, and I have come down to deliver them . . .'" (Exod. 3:7-8). God addressed Israel's needs: You don't have to live like this. Again, Jesus said "I came that they may have life, and have it abundantly" (John 10:10b), and that saying is very important here. The church takes an interest in people like Christ did—for we are the body of Christ.

Cesar Romero, World Vision Colombia's director, reflects: "The surprise is in comparing the past and the present. This was a very individualistic community, with tremendous delinquency. Every sort of delinquency was present: child, youth, adult and drug sales. And to see what is happening now! The action of the liberating gospel of Jesus Christ has succeeded in penetrating to the interior of this community and producing these changes."

On the one hand, the ministries and models of Father Navarro in *La Parroquia de la Ascención* and of Pastor Paniagua in the *Centro* are very much alike. Both leaders demonstrate the strong interpersonal skills of natural leadership, and both show evidence of a strong vision for holistic ministry. On the other hand, however, they are also very different. Navarro implements his vision in a highly organized context. Paniagua implements his in a context that contains far fewer resources, using a catch-as-catch-can approach in the barrios around Soacha.

History

Javier Paniagua is in his forties, a thinker and networker, a resident of San Mateo. The networking gifts showed themselves first, as his mentor, Julio Paucar, explains:

> I was a shoemaker living in San Fernando, a neighborhood of Bogota. I knew Javier's father. When Javier was 10, his father invited me to do something with Javier, as he was getting involved with delinquents. I taught him shoemaking. He came to know shoemaking and Jesus Christ. So now he's a theologian and a shoemaker. We have seen that the gospel makes a person extraordinarily great in the hands of the Lord.

Javier had been preparing for seminary teaching (and is currently teaching Greek and Hebrew for a local seminary). "I came to San Mateo to reopen the church as a favor to a friend while they were seeking a permanent pastor. I had no interest in becoming the pastor. I didn't like how the pastoral system worked." Javier's initial months at San Mateo showed him that the "pastoral system" was not of interest to the neighborhood. The church had closed because of the conduct of the last pastor. Another Protestant church offering salvation in the world to come attracted little positive attention in a barrio still trying to make this world work. The church was attracting negative attention—as the chants of the neighborhood children and the broken windows attested.

Pastora Hernandez was a member of San Mateo before the Paniaguas arrived. She remembers well the beginnings of the work, the purchase of the church site. But the work soon ran aground. Nevertheless, Pastora continued to pray that the work would not die. When the Paniaguas arrived, they were starting not from scratch, but from considerably behind scratch. For four months no one joined in worship.

Javier and Flor, his wife, settled into the community and started teaching shoemaking and hairdressing, started "seeking the *shalom*" of San Mateo. "Settling in" meant many decisions about how they would identify with the marginal standard of living in the community. Javier dresses simply, keeping dress shirts and ties for his seminary work. Friends fixed up their home against Javier's objections. Cesar recalls "When World Vision began to work with them, they were living in terrible conditions. Javier didn't want help—to avoid being separated from the community. We finally persuaded him to accept the help by arguing that we were giving it to his wife and children, not him."

As a result of identifying both with the community and ministry in the community, others began to discover in the *Centro* an instrument for their own response to God's call. The following stories of Rodrigo, Alberto, Carmenza and Luis demonstrate Javier's and Flor's empowerment of local leadership.

Rodrigo Arango has been working with the *Centro* for only three months. He has lived in San Mateo for two years since coming from Ciudad Latina, and shows deep concern for the needs and stability of the barrio. The *Centro*'s tangible responses to the community's needs have attracted his attention. "Too many institutions are deceiving the people. Even the churches mostly care only about a beautiful building or a beautiful worship service, without seeking to respond to the needs of the community." A day laborer, Rodrigo is focusing on home improvement efforts.

Alberto Mejilla is a lay leader. He had been an evangelical for years, but was dissatisfied. His desire had been to be a missionary—which he thought meant working in another country. "Javier helped me expand my understanding of mission. I've been working here now for two years, in the barrios of Bosa, Cristalina and Ricaurte." For Alberto, part of serving as a lay leader means teaching construction and shoemaking.

Carmenza Ramirez is a lay leader, and the mother of Sonja, World Vision Colombia's liaison officer with the *Centro*. She was active for years in the Catholic church, but felt something lacking in her discipleship. "What have I done for others?" she asked herself. About five years ago she suffered a bad fall, with a slow recovery accompanied by much pain and medication. Praying, she experienced God's healing. Earlier this year, she was healed of a serious heart condition. These healings have instilled deep faith and confidence in Carmenza. One of Carmenza's first encounters with the San Mateo church was a prayer meeting during which people prayed for a small burro for transportation. This initially struck her as very strange, but subsequently she decided that this was the sort of engagement of faith with life she had been seeking. She started teaching classes in candymaking at several *centros* (smaller places of activity started by the *Centro*) soon thereafter.

Luis Bellido Peniano comes from a Pentecostal background. At his previous church he was responsible for giving to those in need. When a family's home burned down, Luis wanted to help. But his pastor responded: "To help people makes the church become like an assistance center and the church can't respond to everyone's needs." Luis is now at the *Centro*.

Julio Paucar, Javier's mentor, shares the goals of the *Centro*'s work in one of the neighborhoods: "The principal aim is to bring people to the feet of the Lord Jesus Christ. Further, we desire with the help of the Lord and good hearts and the many offerings that they've made to improve the dwellings of many poor people. Their homes are in very bad—if not inhuman—shape."

Rodrigo, Alberto, Carmenza and Luis: their stories suggest the convergence of the vision that drives the *Centro*. This is important for two reasons. First, it prevents misunderstanding the *Centro* as simply a product of Javier's vision. Javier is a charismatic leader with a strong and well-articulated vision, which might raise the question of whether that vision co-opts other people's agendas. The stories of the other leaders show that for them San Mateo is important as a way of responding to a call of God they had been hearing for some time. Second, it reminds us that holistic ministry is more than word+deed+sign. These stories suggest that another important dimension is a convergence of concern and vision on the part of participants. And in the case of the *Centro*, the participants are becoming leaders.

Leadership

Javier describes these leaders:

They are simple people with no special preparation, whether biblical or secular. They are persons who have accepted Jesus Christ as their Savior, have experienced something of his life and wish to share this experience with others. Their formation has been within the normal activities of our church, which has to do with work in favor of the community with its different needs. So they have understood that the church has a responsibility for the education of the community. It has a responsibility in the formation of the people so that they learn and work at something worthwhile. And it has a responsibility in the organization of the community for the search to improve its life in a program of work with health, nutrition, mutual aid. The church must integrate itself in the community to work for the improvement of the integral family.

They are people who work in secular work and give part of their time to this work. As for their costs [costs related to their work for the *Centro*]—they are paying them out of their own pockets.

Describing what he looks for in emerging leaders, Javier continues:

> Qualities of leaders? They are Christians, consecrated and with a good capacity to service. They understand the redemptive purpose of God for humanity. This is not simply to liberate humanity from condemnation, but also to give them a new life, completely joyful. People without expectations of a good salary. Persons with a good testimony, full of faith.
>
> There are different models of ministry. Some think that being a pastor requires formal study, and so on. But this model—exemplified by Carmenza—is appropriate too: sharing with others what God has done in her life. This is an adequate basis for beginning ministry.
>
> They've had one to two years of participating in our church, and now are going out to other places. Much of their work is at the beginning stages. Now we're giving classes in Bible and theology.

While Javier does not mention it as a requirement, his leaders all have skills that they can teach within the community. Thus, Julio's initial pattern of teaching Javier shoemaking and discipleship is being reproduced in the second generation of leaders.

Javier is currently training the leaders two days a week in a program linked with the *Seminario Crece de Quito*. "Our vision is a seminary here that would provide everything that the leaders need to receive."

Part of the training is how to bring resources to bear on the needs of the community. This involves, for instance, learning how to work more effectively with the government's *madre comunitarias* (community mothers) who start and monitor child care facilities. On the other hand, pushing the envelope of faith receives its due as well. Pastora Hernandez recalls the steps of faith when they started work on sanctuary improvements not knowing how they would meet the costs. Anyhow, the leaders are to be servants of the community. They are not to manage money, whether it is the community's or the church's.

Cesar, World Vision Colombia's director, comments: "All his [Javier's] leaders are from the community. Dangerous! But the Spirit is present. One has to accept that the community has all that it needs within itself. This breaks with much of what has been written regarding development. . . . Javier is neither a preacher nor a teacher. He works, teaches, learns with the people. His educative system is to work with them, to teach doing it with them. It is a family ministry. Javier learned from Flor what he knows about areas like day care. Javier doesn't play an instrument, but his son does."

The Ministry Model

The ministry model calls for houses of prayer and multiple small congregations (*centros*) scattered throughout the barrios rather than a single large church. Javier explains: "There should be no more than 50 people in one location. If the task were simply preaching, a congregation of 5,000 or more would be possible. The point is not to have church buildings, but homes in which we can do our work." Here function (mission) drives form.

The *centros* devote time to corporate prayer. All are welcome. Petitions are usually recorded in a log, and highlighted when answered. Javier says, "People learn that prayer for specific needs makes sense. This awakens a sense of the spiritual." Luis adds, "We start by giving thanks, we use the psalms, bring our petitions. We give testimony to answers to prayer. This is our method of evangelism."

Again, the people consult Scripture on a variety of topics. "People wanted to know what the Bible said about running a home," Flor relates, "so we read Proverbs 31. That led to other questions. With this openness to the Bible, there's no need to force the issue of the gospel."

Worship blends formal and informal elements. When it comes to music, the relevant dangers are of being too restrictive (legalistic) on the one hand or too extreme or manipulative on the other. A Catholic participant feels at home: "It's something like Catholic charismatic worship." As to setting, the usual line between "sacred" and "secular" is intentionally blurred. Javier explains:

> Pastors here usually see churches as holy places in which activities other than worship are improper. When we started giving classes in shoemaking or hairdressing in the church, other pastors said we were desecrating the church.

Where does the *Centro* establish these houses of prayer and the small congregations? Right now they seem to follow the movings of leaders in San Mateo—and the moves are frequent. Also, according to Javier, "We enter communities where there are no ministries directed toward the poor."

Effects

A convenience store

Just down the street from the *Centro*, two women proudly run a small convenience store. They started with a charcoal grill Javier got for them. The grill was for cooking *arepas*, thick soft corn tortillas that are popular snacks in the neighborhood. After a few months, they opened the convenience store. What they do not say—but Javier recounts later—is that they are also contributing generously to *Centro* projects such as the day care center in Cristalina.

The potter's house

Near the *Centro* in another direction is the home of Fabio Meza, the potter. Fabio started with strong prejudices against the evangelicals. He was living in a shack in very poor conditions. Javier recalls: "It looked so unpromising that I wasn't going to knock on the door. But Flor insisted that we knock on his door." Fabio had long been fighting health and financial problems. He was consulting a witch, who was telling him that his problems were due to a third person. The witch said he needed to kill this person to solve his problems. As for finances, at that point Fabio was about to lose his small plot of land. "He didn't want anything to do with us," Javier continues. "But we asked his permission to pray, and over the next year he learned to pray. He learned to pray before he became a Christian. His financial situation improved significantly. When things were really going badly physically, he set himself to fast and pray. He slept long, and on awakening Sunday, got up and brought his whole family to the church." Fabio contributes to the life of the *Centro* in a variety of ways, including preparing people for baptism. He comments on the importance of what is happening in San Mateo:

> Because you're poor, people often don't look at you. The one who has money—that one gets respect although they go against the poor. Now, no. We're all equal. In the gospel some are not seen as great and others as little; all are equal.

The student center in Cristalina

A small prefabricated home at the edge of Cristalina houses the newly-formed *Centro Estudiantil* (student center). The center provides schooling and day care for up to 25 children between six and thirteen years old. The next nearest school is three kilometers away. The alternative for the children is either being alone at home or taking to the streets. At home, the dominant danger is fire from unsupervised use of the stoves. Burns are common, and loss of home or even life are frequent.

The vision for the Student Center is Javier's. The home belongs to Javier's sister; the staff is composed of volunteers. Donations from local residents, both members and nonmembers of the San Mateo *Centro* ("We are teaching the community to give too!"), and a small weekly fee paid by the students' parents cover the Center's costs. The staff provides meals, relying heavily on Colombiorina, a cereal-based drink designed as a nutritional supplement. Javier's brother, Jaime, a resident of Cristalina, brings in the water.

The home also serves as the site for weekly worship (Sunday and Tuesday) and a weekly service of prayer and teaching (Saturday). Alberto is pastor for the growing congregation.

Javier has been working three years to awaken churches in Bogota to the need here in Cristalina. Recently, one church expressed interest in contributing people and other resources to support the work. This is what Javier is looking for: not simply finances, but the involvement of a church as a part of its ongoing conversion. Javier is currently working to gather support for a second building that could house a nursery school and other services.

The housing project

> The first step is organizing the people so that they can identify their needs, their problems, their resources. We're trying to show them that an individualistic way of thinking doesn't help. (Javier)

If funds can be gathered, work on building new homes or improvements to existing ones will start with thirty families in Cristalina and six families in Tesoro. The work in Cristalina will be done with Habitat for Humanity.

The vision

"We encourage people to share a little of their life," says Javier, "while making it clear that this 'little' can be quite a bit.

The story of the Good Samaritan is the best model of ministry we have. He sacrificed time, goods, money and even his security (was he the one, others could well wonder, who attacked the Jew in the first place?!)."

"People often talk about evangelism and social action as two separate things," Javier continues. "Our way of being church is to identify ourselves with the needs, hurts, conflicts, joys and sorrows of other people, so that it's not a question of improving *their* situation, but of improving *our* situation. Through this way of being church we proclaim the faith."

Javier also supports traditional evangelism in cooperation with other churches, and in planning an evangelism campaign with an imported evangelist. Nevertheless, this type of evangelization seems dehumanizing to him: "I don't want to organize churches that simply sing and pray, but churches responding to the needs of the community."

When participants turn to Scripture to make sense of what happens at the *Centro*, they cite many texts familiar in the evangelical rediscovery of holistic ministry. But participants also draw on a broader range of texts, including the following passages:

> "You are the light of the world. A city set on a hill cannot be hid. Nor do men light a lamp and put it under a bushel, but on a stand, and it gives light to all in the house. Let your light so shine before men, that they may see your good works and give glory to your Father who is in heaven. (Matt. 5:14-16)

> "Woe to you, scribes and Pharisees, hypocrites! for you tithe mint and dill and cumin, and have neglected the weightier matters of the law, justice and mercy and faith; these you ought to have done, without neglecting the others. (Matt. 23:23)

> "You yourselves know that these hands ministered to my necessities, and to those who were with me. In all things I have shown you that by so toiling one must help the weak, remem-

bering the words of the Lord Jesus, how he said, 'It is more blessed to give than to receive.'" (Acts 20:34-35)

But the free gift is not like the trespass. For if many died through one man's trespass, much more have the grace of God and the free gift in the grace of that one man Jesus Christ abounded for many. (Rom. 5:15)

For we are his workmanship, created in Christ Jesus for good works, which God prepared beforehand, that we should walk in them. (Eph. 2:10)

who gave himself for us to redeem us from all iniquity and to purify for himself a people of his own who are zealous for good deeds. (Titus 2:14)

One result of the ministries inspired by this vision is that additional neighborhoods have invited the *Centro Nazareno San Mateo* to start *centros* in their areas too. This sort of invitation is rarely given, especially considering that this is a traditionally Catholic country.

A second result is that the *Centro* has enriched other church and parachurch groups in the greater Bogota area. "We have learned more from them than they have from us," testifies Cesar, World Vision Colombia's director. "The first facilitator assigned to the San Mateo project has since left World Vision Colombia to start his own typesetting business. But he's still supporting the San Mateo project through donating typesetting services. That's the sort of involvement we desire from all our facilitators."

Theological and Missiological Reflections

In the *Centro*, how do evangelism, social action and openness to the Spirit interrelate? These categories are somewhat artificial in relation to the *Centro's* actual practice. The primary expression of the mission is active solidarity with the people of the neighborhood. Characteristically, this means networking and organizing to address common concerns and prayer. *Centro* members pray for the whole spectrum of people's needs—needs for which organizing is an appropriate response, and needs for which it is not (e.g., untreatable illnesses). The lives of the *Centro* members, particularly their commitment to the good of the neighborhood, raise questions in the neighborhood—questions to which their testimony of their encounter with the God who notes and responds to people's needs is the only adequate response.

Is it appropriate to call this an incarnational ministry model? With the exception of the Paniaguas, leadership is indigenous. On the other hand, we would not want to underestimate the importance of Javier and Flor's modeling of "downward mobility" that sets an example for others to follow.

The ministry here has much in common with other holistic ministries among the poor. It also contrasts, however, with some of these at two points. First, it contrasts with community organizing models in which prayer plays a less central role. This is not to side with San Mateo as a privileged expression of spirituality. There are, presumably, multiple ways in which the spirituality of a ministering community focused on community organizing may find expression. Rather, it is to highlight the central role of prayer both as a "method" of addressing problems and as a fundamental expression of reliance on God.

Second, San Mateo contrasts with evangelism models in which the "spiritual needs" of the community are addressed first and, subsequently, other sorts of needs. Viv Grigg, who has practiced and promoted holistic ministry primarily in Asia, has created a model that appears to favor this approach. Grigg questions whether there are alternative models that can lead to the creation and sustaining of churches. San Mateo would appear to be one such model.

How does San Mateo relate to "liberation theology"? The question poses itself, given the frequent references to Exodus in the church's self-presentation. A full answer to this question would take too much time, primarily because it would demand some unpacking of the multiple theological and missiological options associated with "liberation theology." Nevertheless, the following points are worth noting. Javier reports having encountered multiple liberation themes in his seminary training, and draws on these in explicating the "oppression" of the people or the identity of the thieves in John 10. On the other hand, he is not consciously incorporating liberationist responses, perceiving these to be either committed to violence (which he rejects) or too theoretical for the practical needs of his neighbors. Perhaps more important, his model assumes that communities of Christians oriented by the values of the kingdom and practicing small-scale capitalism informed by these same values are the preferred engines for moving their neighborhoods forward.

Mission that integrates word, deed and sign is an important part of the *Centro*'s story. But also of importance is solidarity with one's neighbors, so that one talks of "*our* problems," whether in putting food on the table or discovering God's gracious presence at the table. Equally important is the Paniaguas' empowerment of local leadership, working on the assumption—the faith—that God has already provided the human resources for Soacha's growing neighborhoods.

4

La Parroquia de la Resurrección

L a Parroquia de la Resurrección (The Parish of the Resurrection) lies at the southwest edge of Mexico City. There, in the midst of a poor community of rural emigrants, this church led by Father Alfonso Navarro, MSpS, is being transformed into an active witness to the gospel. Young and old are discovering what their baptism means, and coming to faith in Christ. In tightly knit small groups they are also discovering what faithfulness to Christ means, expressed in outreach and service to their neighbors. New life within these groups means new life in the community, through cooperatives, medical and legal clinics, job training and celebration. The Spirit's fruit and gifts inform this work in multiple ways.

Father Navarro's parish is located in Pedregal de San Nicolás in Tlalpan. Here the plain rises into the mountains, and people call the area Ajusco, the name of a nearby peak. About 40,000 people live in the parish area. Settlement in the region began not long ago, and people are still coming from other parts of Mexico City and the Republic. Housing ranges from small, well-cared-for homes to cardboard shacks. Some roads are paved. Ninety percent of the population would be at the minimum salary level or below; 10 percent would be in the lower middle class. While 90 percent of school-age children are in school, 35 percent of the men and 5 percent of the women have had no schooling. Work often means traveling long distances, and youth gangs are a growing problem. Signs of hope and despair compete for attention.

La Parroquia de la Resurrección has become the flagship for SINE (Sistema Integral de la Nueva Evangelización, i.e., Systematic and Integral New Evangelization), Father Navarro's program for parishes. SINE is used in over 500 parishes in thirteen countries throughout the Americas, with about fifty parishes added to the program each year. Recently, SINE teams have begun work with Catholic schools. Father Navarro and his team provide support through consultations, retreats and seminars, coordination of missions, publications and audio and video resources. The story of SINE's development starts before that of the parish, so I will start with SINE and then move to the parish. In terms of the "word-work-wonder" issue that informs this book, the movement of the history traced here is from "wonder" to "word" to "work."

SINE

In 1971, a team from Melodyland, a Protestant ministry based in Southern California (U.S.A.), led a conference on charismatic renewal at San José del Altillo, the center for the order of the Misioneros del Espíritu Santo (Missionaries of the Holy Spirit) in Mexico City. The site was appropriate. Missionaries of the Holy Spirit is an indigenous order founded as one of five Works of the Cross (Obras de la Cruz) in response to visions Señora Concepción Cabrera received early in this century. After the conference, Father Navarro, a member of the Misioneros, was asked by his superiors to oversee the ongoing renewal.

44

The next year, Father Navarro set up a center for renewal. The center was not parish-based, but drew people from all over the city. He gave "Life in the Spirit" seminars, with materials from Word of Life, a Catholic charismatic community in Ann Arbor, Michigan, U.S.A.

In 1973, Father Navarro changed the seminar to a "Basic Evangelism Seminar." The Bible, theology and experience prompted this change, which was less a split from and more a contextualization of the charismatic movement. Scholars such as C.H. Dodd were stressing the difference in the early church between announcing the gospel and teaching about the gospel. Shouting "Fire!" is different from lecturing on the effects of fire on the body. The "Life in the Spirit" seminars, Father Navarro decided, assumed an already-received announcement. Father Navarro's experience suggested that many in the seminars had not heard the announcement.

In 1974 Father Navarro began to work beyond Mexico City, with seminars in other parts of Mexico and the Americas. The center continued its program, evolving toward what is now known as SINE. But Father Navarro believed it had a limited impact because it lay outside the normal framework of Catholic life and nurture—the parish. He requested, and received from his bishop, a parish territory as a pilot project for SINE. Thus in 1981 Father Navarro became the parish priest for *La Parroquia de la Resurrección*.

Father Navarro thinks that SINE should interest the priest of a traditional parish. In his view, the traditional parish is a "service station" for the 99 percent of the parish who appear only when they need services such as a baptism or a marriage. Perhaps one percent are committed, often expressing this through various groups that may draw them away from parish life. In contrast to the parable of the lost sheep, the priest of a traditional parish spends his time with the committed one while the 99 are left wandering! The low level of giving also means that the priest must devote time to holding private masses, raffles and so on to make ends meet. Reorganizing a parish along the lines of SINE addresses these problems. The 99 percent get attention; the remaining 1 percent contributes to parish life. The percentages begin to change, and increased giving reduces the economic scramble. As Father Navarro says, "Like the parable of the Lost Sheep, the pastor and the newly evangelized go to find the sheep. Use the feet, not the seat! From pews to shoes!"

SINE aims to create and sustain the parish as an evangelizing community. SINE has four major elements: preparation, evangelism, growth and follow-up, and social action. The program adds these elements in that order as a parish undergoes the conversion from a traditional parish to an evangelizing community. Subsequently, all the elements are present in each community. But what does this involve?

Preparation

Preparation leads up to evangelism, and involves various methods of initial contact. The usual method is the unmethodical testimony of the evangelized to their peers. Other methods include mass media and executives' breakfasts. An annual evangelizing mission visits every home in the parish area.

At the parish level, the parish area is broken down into units (sectors, subsectors, blocks) for face-to-face pastoral care. A questionnaire is used to learn about the people's lives. Finally, those who will do the evangelism are mobilized and trained.

The gospel is shared and response invited at this stage. A common tool is the tract *¿Ya lo tienes tu?* ("Do you have it [a living encounter with Jesus for a new life]?"). The tract uses pictures and Bible verses, and concludes with a suggested prayer of commitment. Since people often see themselves as Christian solely on the basis of baptism, however, SINE speaks of responders as "touched," rather than "evangelized."

Evangelism

Evangelism announces the Good News and calls for a response. It occurs in a formal setting over an extended period of time (at least 30 hours). The time allows for a careful presentation of the gospel, and ample opportunity for the participants to explore its meaning for themselves.

The goals of evangelism are conversion, acceptance of Jesus as Savior, surrendering to Jesus as Lord and receiving the Spirit. In sacramental terms, and in a context in which most have already been baptized and confirmed, the goals of evangelism are the renewal of one's baptism and confirmation. The end result (not, strictly speaking, a part of evangelism) is a deepening of the meaning of participating in the Eucharist. The table on page 48 (Figure 4.1) shows the content and sacramental linkages of evangelism in SINE.

Some people tend to play evangelism off against the sacraments ("living faith" versus "dead ritual"). Because of this, SINE's reconnection of faith and sacrament is a central contribution of this model.

Growth and Follow-up

Growth and follow-up include discipleship and the apostolate. The major emphases of discipleship are small communities, teaching and the sharing of one's goods.

The small communities (*pequeñas comunidades parroquiales*) are formed only from the newly-evangelized. These groups meet weekly for praise, teaching and application. The application consists of either "edification" (concerning the spiritual, religious, ecclesial, eternal) or "solidarity" (concerning the material, social, secular, temporal). Typically, three weeks a month are devoted to spiritual edification and one week to social solidarity, but the small group's circumstances may dictate a change.

The small communities are the primary place for teaching and for members to study together. SINE prepares all the materials used for this study process—six years' worth of curriculum and growing.

SINE encourages members of the small communities to share their possessions, both material and spiritual (*comunicación cristiana de bienes*). The sovereignty of the Creator over the world and things, the lordship of Jesus over us and over all

Figure 4.1: The content and sacramental linkages of evangelism in SINE

Sacrament	Announcement	Exhortation	Expression of the Response
Renewal of Baptism	The love of the Father Salvation in Jesus • Sin and its consequences • Jesus, God's solution	Accept Jesus as Savior Be converted and return to God Renounce Satan and his works Be born of the Spirit	Liturgy of Penance
Renewal of Confirmation	The Lordship of Jesus The Promise of the Father The Gift of the Spirit A New Pentecost—now	The promise is for you—now!	Liturgy of Consecration
Community-centered in the Eucharist	[None, since the announcement has already been given.]	Remain and persevere • In church and community • In the Word and the teaching • Praying always in the Spirit • Carrying the cross daily • Being witnesses to the Resurrected Lord	Liturgy of the Eucharist

things and the Christian vision of the use of goods and property undergird this sharing. Members are encouraged to tithe, to discern what is necessary and what is superfluous in their lives and to strive for a simpler, more sober and more austere lifestyle. They are then encouraged to allocate the superfluous to savings, to needs inside the parish community and to needs outside the parish community. This encourages continual discernment, rather than simply following a set of formulas.

"Apostolate" is the term for service inside the church (see Eph. 4:12). SINE expects the evangelized to give four hours each week to ministry. This is the "tithe" of time, matching the tithe of income. As Father Navarro says, "You work forty hours to build Egypt; work four hours to build the Kingdom!" Part- or full-time service, whether for a definite or indefinite period of time, is also encouraged. The success of SINE depends on substantial response to this invitation, particularly among the consecrated—those making an open-ended full-time commitment.

Service takes many forms. Pastoral activity may mean participation in evangelistic retreats, seminars or worship; or supervision of catechesis, the small communities or sectors of the parish. Social action includes all of the programs the parish carries out. Ministry support ranges from recordkeeping and other administrative support to the various ministries, to creating written and audiovisual resources.

Social Action

Social action simply continues, on the one hand, the responses to problems that occur within the small communities. On the other hand, it is a further step, for it addresses not only the needs in the small communities, but also the needs in the sector or even the entire parish area.

The small communities are the primary base for social action. This is not because they or their members are the primary agents of social action, although this is also often true. This is because the small communities are to be themselves models of hope. According to Father Navarro, the goal is to "show to the world alternative solutions to the problems of people and of the world."

A range of actions are necessary. Assistential action meets urgent and immediate needs. Promotional action helps individuals or groups gain access to needed skills or resources and become self-sufficient. Structural action addresses the institutions or structures of society. Moving along this range makes the question of roles (who does what) become increasingly important.

Assistential activity is necessary even when promotional and structural forms of social action also come into play. Food banks and medical and dental clinics are examples of assistential activity. The danger of abuse, however, means assistance must be temporary and, when possible, should be given in exchange for community service.

Examples of promotional activity include work clearinghouses, credit unions, family gardens, small animal husbandry and consumer or producer cooperatives. Teaching (literacy and job training) is another major form of promotional activity. It is appropriate, Father Navarro argues, for the parish to promote such activity and help to get it started. Maintaining these activities is the laity's responsibility.

As for structural activity, SINE distinguishes between activity inside and outside the parish territory. Inside, the church may promote various actions. Outside, the church's responsibility is to pass on the church's social teachings to form the consciences of the laity. The laity, in turn, bring these teachings to bear in their own situations, whether at work or through political organizations. But the church should avoid partisan political positions, a restriction that also applies to the small communities. As Father Navarro puts it, "Sometimes in the churches we stay only in assistential levels or deal with emergencies—earthquakes, flooding, wars. Promotional activity is better, and structural change is best, but without ideologizing, without radicalizing, without the 'isms'."

A parish using the SINE model in Juárez, Chihuahua, shows one way this works. One of its small communities reflected a few years back on the need for Christian values in local politics. One of the members, Francisco Barrio, decided to run for the mayor's office. Unsuccessful in getting PRI's (*Partido Revolucionario Institucional* or the Institutional Revolutionary Party, Mexico's ruling party) backing, he ran under PAN's (*Partido Acción Nacional* or the National Action Party, an opposition party) banner—and won. Raúl Matienzo's account of subsequent events shows the type of faith and politics questions with which he and other members of the small communities have to deal:

> Barrio was recently criticized because in the ceremony *El Grito* ["The Shout"] the past fifteenth of September [Mexico's Independence Day], he led cheers not only for the [traditional] heroes, but also for the Virgin of Guadalupe. His view is that this is not inserting religion in an official observance, but simply being more faithful to Hidalgo's original shout [*El Grito*]. [Hidalgo was a priest, and his shout, which drew deeply from Mexican spirituality, launched the Mexican revolution. —Ed.] In the last few months he moved to a house located in one of the poorest sections of Juárez. As a result, some conservatives accused him of being a communist in sheep's clothing, and the leftists, on their part, said that he was a fascist demagogue.

La Parroquia de la Resurrección

What does the "Systematic and Integral New Evangelization" (SINE) program look like in practice? An obvious place to look is the Parish of the Resurrection.

Father Navarro is the parish priest, and in this traditional role oversees the life of the parish. Nontraditionally, he does this with a team of seventy full-time lay workers, aided by many others working part-time or giving their "tithe" of time. The parish is broken down into sectors, subsectors and blocks, with workers responsible for the people in their area. One worker is responsible for the families and persons living on each street. A major responsibility of these workers is visiting each home throughout the year. Maps of the sectors are distributed, to which parishioners point with pride: "I am here. I belong to this sector and I belong to this parish."

At the same time that the parish uses and serves as a test site for SINE, it also uses the resources of the five *Obras de la Cruz* (Works of the Cross—two of which are named below). In 1985, for instance, sixteen of the most developed small communities became part of *El Apostolado de la Cruz* (Apostolate of the Cross). Since then, the number of groups participating has more than doubled. This *Obra de la Cruz* is an order for all Christians; its goal is that people will know and experience the spirituality of Christ the Priest and Victim, and know the salvific value of suffering accepted with love. That same year, eighty of those serving full-time became part of *La Alianza de Amor* (Covenant of Love). This *Obra de la Cruz* gathers laity who commit themselves to experience profoundly the spirituality of Jesus the Priest and Victim and to carry out an active ministry within their own station in life.

Expressions of Community

Community life in the parish finds expression in a variety of forms, including worship, the small communities and the groups taking responsibility for various parts of the parish program. Presently there are approximately 100 small communities, with six to eighteen people per group. While the program is uniform, different groups have different histories, and develop different emphases as well.

Sister Emma Marie belongs to one of these groups, which meets in the evening in the modest home of one of its members.

On a typical evening, thirteen or so people fill the living and dining rooms. Some are teenagers, others are close to retirement. The opening singing is enthusiastic, the songs familiar from other settings. Their prayers offer up individual and group joys, fears and needs. The group works through the evening's lesson at a relaxed pace, their conversation punctuated by laughter often prompted by standing jokes. People are comfortable with each other. Calendars and pencils come out at the meeting's close as they review coming events and coordinate responsibilities.

How does the sharing of goods work in this community? Some who are well-off take care of the needs of another family in which one spouse is committed to full-time service and the other to half-time service. Personal austerity is promoted. People are encouraged to give away things they have not used within the past year. "They tell me," says Sr. Emma Marie, 'How does it look? Should I keep this, or give it away? Because I haven't used it for a year. Maybe I should start using it.' That's a practical thing."

Evangelism, growth and follow-up

Within the parish, about 200 persons per year are evangelized in the seminars. A number of factors affect how people respond to the parish's evangelism and discipling. More women than men participate in the small communities (76 percent of the adults, 60 percent of the youth). The state from which people have come is a factor; those from the central area tend to be more responsive than those from the southwest, where folk religion is stronger.

Different methods for those in different social strata are needed (both here and in other parishes). While lower-income groups are open to door-to-door visits, this approach meets resistance elsewhere ("I'm too busy"). In these cases, the team may hold breakfasts or dinners in which they present the gospel.

Dealing with substance abusers (e.g., drug addicts) requires a different approach. Teams make initial contact on the street, sometimes using street theater. They invite people who show interest to coffee houses to continue conversations. Mike O'Shaughnessy, a Baptist pastor who formerly worked with Teen Challenge, headed up this rehabilitation work for a time.

Of those who go through the fundamental evangelism, about 60 percent stay actively involved, although this means a significant commitment. The time commitment, for instance, is at least a daily private devotional time, the weekly three-hour small group meeting, a four-hour "tithe" of time to apostolic service and attending Mass. The 40 percent who stop participating actively do so largely because of the high demands. As SINE takes this pattern of active involvement to follow directly from the nature of discipleship, there is no attempt to design a "lite" track. Rather, workers regularly encourage the inactive evangelized to return to active parish life.

Parish social action

Starting with assistential forms, the parish has for a number of years held a "Week of Solidarity." The parish recently changed the name to "Week of Charity" after the government started using "solidarity" for its own programs. Matienzo described it for us:

> It was a week in which all the consecrated would devote themselves to social action, to give emphasis to this aspect of ministry. For example, if some were carpenters, they would offer that work for the people who had a problem in that area. Instead of going to each house to give the announcement [of the gospel] as we do in the missions, we went to offer "In what way can I serve you?" The people were very surprised at first; they didn't know what to do. But some of them took it seriously, and they'd say "Well, I haven't washed my clothes and I haven't washed my dishes, so you can help me with that." There were pro-

grams to plant trees, and the local government added campaigns for literacy programs and vaccinations—also for the dogs.

Ongoing projects include a clearing-house for jobs and a medical dispensary. The parish monitors local health providers to assure quality medical care for the poor, and works with other agencies to help professionals offer their services to the community. For instance, one day each week two lawyers give consultations free of charge.

Turning to promotional forms, examples of projects include a carpentry school and home construction. The school of carpentry aims both to train and to make furniture of suitable design and price for Ajusco. At this point those heading the project have acquired a building and a number of machines.

The construction project helps people upgrade their homes. Father Navarro describes the poorest areas: "When they have only one room, the parents, the children, the stove, the pig and the chicken all live together. Sometimes the house is built with cardboard. . . . But I say new man, new house. A son of the King can't live in a pigsty." The project goal is to build 1,000 homes. The project provides a variety of basic home plans; those who will live in the homes provide a significant portion of the labor. But a lack of funds has slowed progress.

Since 1987, the parish has worked in cooperation with World Vision Mexico to operate a number of day care centers for families whose children need care during the day.

A recent dispute over milk prices at a local store shows how the small communities address community issues. In Mexico, the government provides milk for sale at a reduced price. A local merchant was selling it at this price only if people bought other items at his store. A number of small communities talked over the problem together and met with the merchant—unsuccessfully. Later, more of the small communities met to discuss the problem. The merchant's supervisor happened to be present at this meeting, and promised publicly to solve the problem, which he did.

Linkages

What links between word, work and wonder are evident in SINE and in *La Parroquia de la Resurrección*?

Evangelism and the teaching that follows it clearly lead to a variety of forms of social action. The small communities seem to be the primary place for this. In these small groups, members receive and reflect on teaching related to living out their faith in all spheres of life—including their work. There members deepen their understanding and experience of what sharing means, so that sharing may come to include their goods. The small communities are also a place to reflect politically, to the point that SINE finds it necessary to stress the distinction between a small group and a political action group.

Social action, on the other hand, is one context in which evangelism may spontaneously occur. A woman heard of SINE and, impressed, offered to drive some distance to teach dressmaking. After a few classes she was visibly discouraged at the students' difficulty in learning. They responded by evangelizing her. Later, she was proudly showing the work some of the students had done, and planning was underway to set up a number of workshops for making dresses. Generally, the many forms of social action started by the parish seem to create a good climate for explicit evangelizing efforts.

The charismatic renewal that started all this is more a matter of environment than program. That is, there is no charismatic emphasis corresponding to the evangelism and social action emphases. Nevertheless, its presence is palpable. The tract *¿Ya lo tienes tu?* provides us with an example. It concludes not only with the need for conversion, but also with the need to be born of and filled with the Spirit. The tract adds a prayer to the Spirit for a new birth to the suggested prayer of conversion to Jesus.

A second area in which the renewal is very evident is worship. Nightly meetings for prayer and singing (the first hour) and the Eucharist (the second hour) precede major feasts in the Christian calendar. In the first hour, a worship leader leads in prayer, meditation and singing. The singing may be quiet or exuberant, with arms raised in petition and praise. Nevertheless, while the influence of the charismatic renewal—respecter of neither national nor denominational boundaries—is much in evidence, equally in evidence is a deeply-rooted indigenous spirituality. The songs may be universal; the pictures dominating the parish sanctuary are highly particular: the Virgin of Guadalupe, the Sacred Heart as it appeared to Señora Concepción Cabrera.

And who gathers in this worship? Young and old are there. Some wear the clothes of the modern office, others the clothes of the farm. The worship leader was, not too long ago, offering up his arms to various drugs. The ancient prayer "Come, Holy Spirit" is on the way to being answered.

Conclusion

This section speaks to two questions. First, how does this model present a picture of holism? Second, what is particularly important about this model?

In what respects is this model holistic?

The Christian community is a sign of hope, a sign of the kingdom. The community is a sign of hope both in the new life in the small communities and in the ministry of the church in the parish area. This occurs in dramatic ways in the rehabilitation work with drug addicts. There the move into the community may be literally a move from death into life. It happens more subtly as the community develops new ways of dealing with questions of possessions and power. Turning to the church in ministry to the community, the practice of going door-to-door with the question "How can we help you?" is strong evidence that something new is happening.

Word, work, and wonder are present and integrated. Regarding word, work and wonder, the centerpiece of SINE is evangelism. Subsequent teaching makes it clear that the Christian life—individually and communally—is a life directed toward the neighbor in very concrete ways. Service is an integral part of making disciples. Both in its history and today, the congregation shows multiple signs of the charismatic renewal.

Focusing specifically on "work" (social action), the assistential is best developed, the promotional less so and the structural even less. In part this may reflect the parish's own pilgrimage—what it has learned and what it has yet to learn. In part it reflects ministry models that require resources that are scarce in the community, particularly money. In part it reflects SINE's understanding of the church's role. The church encourages, but is not responsible for, the empowerment of the community itself. That is the responsibility of the people in the community, particularly of the evangelized. Is, then, empowerment going on? The church is providing cohesiveness, which the community would not otherwise have, and the trajectory of church teaching is to encourage multiple small steps toward greater responsibility in the political arena.

Why is La Parroquia de la Resurrección-SINE important?

This model is a contextualization of the charismatic renewal in a context in which nominal Christianity is a danger. As there are few contexts in which nominal Christianity is not a danger, Father Navarro's shift from renewal to basic evangelism merits careful reflection.

This model weaves evangelism into parish life in a variety of ways. It is not that it has developed new methods of evangelism. Rather, the small communities nurture a style of life, a group character, that raises questions among neighbors. Further, dividing the parish into block levels serves an ongoing process of intentional evangelism.

This model holds together the local and the global, the particular and the universal in useful ways. For example, both the indigenous Mexican spirituality represented in Señora Concepción Cabrera and by the modern charismatic renewal inform its spirituality. (Is the story of SINE in part the story of how God used Protestant charismatics from Southern California to awaken Catholic charismatics in Mexico?) Again, in ecumenical issues, the model views the activities of preparation, evangelism and social action as areas for common witness, and it welcomes cooperation with Protestants. But it also acknowledges the need for each tradition to handle growth and follow-up according to its own lights.

Further, this model promotes lay ministry in the parish within a traditional Catholic framework. While the parish priest (*párroco*) retains his full authority, this model acknowledges and unleashes a wide range of gifts within that framework.

The *La Parroquia de la Resurrección-SINE* model integrates concerns that many people and organizations often separate (evangelism, social action, renewal). Even better, it integrates word, sacraments, community and the social in a well-ordered pastoral plan.

5

Scripture Search

Scripture Search is being developed by World Vision in the Philippines[1] as a means of integrating Scripture with community transformation. The question of integrating Scripture into the process of community transformation is important enough to include this study, despite the fact that here the work of the Spirit is not an explicit theme of reflection.

My thanks to the World Vision staff in the Philippines for their hospitality, their assistance in bringing together the material for this case study and their suggestions for revisions. Among the World Vision staff I would like to particularly thank Nora Avarientos, the director at the time I conducted my research, for creating space for this study; Malcolm (Mac) Bradshaw, for many conversations regarding the issues Scripture Search addresses; Bing Abadam and R.J. Salsalida, for introducing me to Scripture Search in Zambales; and Remy Geraldes and Xenia Legaspi, for sharing their experiences of Scripture Search in Metro Manila. May Scripture Search be a continued source of nourishment for them, and for those with whom they work.

Context

Scripture Search has been developed within the context of a number of pilgrimages. Some of the more important ones are:

World Vision's understanding of mission. "World Vision in the Philippines, in obedience to God's call to participate in building His Kingdom, is committed to enable the poor, the marginalized and the oppressed individuals, families and communities to experience God's transformation as envisioned in Isaiah 65:17-25 and to actualize their God-given potential." This mission statement reflects the pilgrimage from working *for* the poor to working *with* the poor.

World Vision's church relations. World Vision has been on a pilgrimage from being an exclusively Protestant organization with a more or less explicit anti-Catholic bias to being an organization in and through which both Catholics and Protestants can engage in mission. This has meant a corresponding pilgrimage from approaches to Scripture that stressed Protestant perspectives over and against Catholic ones and undervalued the spirituality of community members, to approaches that stress common perspectives and build on the spirituality of community members, be they Protestant or Catholic.

World Vision's learning theory. The shift in mission understanding implies a pedagogical shift, which carries over also into the spiritual dimension. Thus a local practitioner said: "With the emergence of a strong emphasis on people participation [and] people management in Better Future projects, an approach to spiritual nurture which emphasizes discovery and sharing was needed." The intention is to move away from keeping the meaning of Scripture in the hands of experts.

Latin American ecclesial base communities. While Scripture Search is an indigenous response to ministry needs in the Philippines, it has obvious affinities with approaches being developed elsewhere, particularly among some of the Catholic base communities in Latin America.

Before turning to three accounts of Scripture Search within the context of World Vision's development work, note that here (and elsewhere) World Vision workers are referred to as "facilitators," and the group of people from the community providing leadership for the World Vision projects is the "core group."

Some Examples

Scripture Search has different faces. Here are some stories that illustrate this variety, starting with an extended description of Scripture Search in the context of one project.

Making and marketing bagoong sauce

The seven women of varying ages beam with pride as they divided equally among themselves the US$71 they gained from their small business. It is worth it, they all chorused, after working hard and waiting for three months. The gain is not enough to make them materially rich. But the experience that goes with it makes them spiritually richer.

"God really rewards the good stewards," says 30-year-old Rene Job Salsalida, a facilitator of a World Vision project assisting the seven women, as he reflects on the Parable of the Talents during the group's project completion report.

The seven women are involved in a *bagoong*-making venture as one of the livelihood projects of the World Vision *Hiyas ng Pag-asa* project in the fishing village of Amungan in Iba, Zambales, 110 kilometers west of the Philippine capital of Manila. *Bagoong* is a native sauce made from fermented anchovy fish. The *bagoong*-making started through a US$178 loan from World Vision. "If God can turn water into wine he surely can turn the anchovy fish into a good-tasting and good-smelling *bagoong*," says 30 year-old Rodemia Aramay, the group's leader and its youngest member.

The group's first *bagoong* is an instant hit in the public market of Iba, Zambales. They have already received several advance orders. This has inspired them to ask for a bigger loan from World Vision for the second phase of their project. "We dream of being the best producer of *bagoong* in the entire province of Zambales," says Macaria Merindo, who at 65 is the oldest in the group. Zambales is known nationally for its high-quality *bagoong*, which pegged a price of US$21 per six-gallon can in the local market. The women are confident they can realize their dream because, as 34-year-old Jean Aramay always says, "our *bagoong* is the best because it is the product of good fermentation and hard prayer."

After mashing, *bagoong* is fermented for a minimum of three months to produce the best results. That long period provides the group with opportunities to work together, pray together and share together their experiences of the Lord. They have regular Bible reflections called Scripture Search during formal meetings led by facilitator Rene Job. This Scripture Search and their interaction give them the opportunities to experience the renewing power of the Word.

Scripture Search, says Malcolm (Mac) Bradshaw, church and community relations coordinator for World Vision in the Philippines, is the bringing of questions from life experience to an appropriate Scripture text. "The objective," he explains, "is to help members of a group understand their situation in the light of a specific Biblical text. This is a prepared study where the following questions are being answered: What are the similarities between our own experience and that of the people in the Bible text we are studying? What light do we get from the Biblical story to help us in our present situation? What should we do about it? [Another way of doing this] is the informal one where someone just brings out a verse during work time as in the case of these seven women sharing the Scripture while mashing the fish."

"The work and Word have united us and given us peace," enthuses 41-year-old Zenaida Fernandez, whose house has become the group's meeting place. The seven women divide the work equally among themselves. Someone buys the fish and salt. Four or five mash the fish and salt. Someone monitors the fermentation process. Another is in charge of sales. "We always work in the spirit of teamwork and trust," says 52-year-old widow Purificacion Castrense.

Rev. Virginio Ducos, pastor of the Amungan Grace Bible Church, World Vision's partner for this project, has seen the growth of the seven women. "They have already outgrown their dole-out mentality. Now, they want to be owners of their development," he says. The earnings the women make from the *bagoong* project are a big help to their fishermen husbands, whose income from fishing can hardly support a big family. "The project has made us productive," says 38-year-old Nelly Manalo, who has five children. Sixty-two-year-old Purita Aramay, who has 10 children and whose husband can no longer work because of sickness, always sheds tears of joy whenever she talks of God's provision. "God is so good to us. My youngest daughter is even graduating this year from college," she says.

The seven women are a source of inspiration to this fishing village of 6,000 people. Not only do they share the Word through their mouth, they share it through their work. "They are our models here," says Rev. Ducos.

Interpersonal relationships

One discussion of how to manage a cooperative was sidetracked when tensions among another group became evident. This group began praying, and in the context of this two-hour prayer meeting people shared their concerns—chiefly, hatred for one member of the core group who had misused funds and committed adultery with someone else in the community. Those praying confessed their having isolated this person, as they had been planning how to remove her from the core group. The group wrestled with how reconciliation might occur. As a result, the member eventually confessed and relinquished her office.

The group has worked since then to help her regain confidence.

A reflection on Luke 9

A group reflected on Luke 9:57-62, particularly on verse 62 ("No one who puts his hand to the plow and looks back is fit for the kingdom of God"). The group decided to role-play the verse. The facilitator recalls: "All members of the working group are women, but for the first time there were two farmers also. So naturally they took the role in verse 62 of a plower and a *carabao* [water buffalo]. To make it realistic, they utilized the available materials and demonstrated the plowing technique. The man who portrayed the *carabao* was very thin, the plower heavy-set. To top it off, the plower started looking back as he plowed, so that he started stumbling into the others seated in the circle, with the *carabao* becoming misguided and losing his way." Ever since, this session has been a graphic reminder of the importance of commitment on the part of the leadership group.

The Model

Scripture Search itself is a way of doing group Bible study, moving from life to Bible, and forming part of the action-reflection cycle[2] that drives community transformation. Fleshing this description out also means describing the strategy of biblical integration, of which Scripture Search is a part, and describing the assumptions underlying Scripture Search.

The strategy

World Vision's strategy for biblical integration contains three major components: Isaiah 65:17-25 as a framework for community planning, the use of Scripture Search to inform the day-to-day decisions of the community, and curricula for more systematic Bible study (Bible-to-Life). Mac Bradshaw wrote the following in an in-house document:[3]

> Three approaches weave together to make up a strategy of biblical integration. First, the Isaiah vision of a new

heaven and new earth (65:17-25) sets our course heading for the goals toward which the Spirit of God is taking the new creation, so we can seek to follow along in our program strategies. Second, cases (events and stories) from the Scriptures which offer analogies to problems which groups of people in the projects are struggling to overcome are reflected upon by the group in the midst of the "action-reflection-action" process. Third, a Biblical curriculum on "wholistic ministry" is made available to the churches in the project areas so that the responsibility for spiritual nurture of their members who are in projects is done in a way that compliments and benefits from the impact of the project in the community.

The Isaiah vision helps the community articulate a comprehensive vision of their desired future. Within the context of this vision the community can address specific issues (health, employment and so on) without losing sight of the long-term goal. The use of Isaiah's vision (the community could perhaps use other texts equally well) encourages the community to attend to the multiple dimensions of this desired future. In Mac Bradshaw's words:

What did the prophet see?

1. He saw a world in which there is no longer death of children due to malnutrition and misfortune.
2. He saw old people "completing their days," living full and fulfilled lives.
3. He saw families secure in their own houses, surrounded by fertile gardens symbolizing sources for health, wholesome environment and sufficient resources for livelihood.
4. He saw restored community and communion. "Before they call . . ." there is unity, harmonious community relationships, prayer in unison, a singularity of heart and purpose. "I will answer them . . ." Fellowship between people and God, which rebellion in Eden shattered, is restored.
5. The peaceful state God originally intended is being restored.

"The wolf and lamb will feed together." Even creation, witnessing mankind being healed, manifests a new congeniality and responsiveness. "They will not destroy or do harm all over My holy mountain," says Yahweh. The world returns to a state of "Shalom" where animals and men cease to exploit one another and wars seem out of place.

The Bible study curriculum used by World Vision in the Philippines is the Institute for Pastoral Development's (IPD) revision and translation of portions of *Training for Community Ministries*, prepared by the Lumko Missiological Institute in South Africa. The IPD is one of the ministries of "The Joy of the Lord Community," the oldest and largest of the Catholic charismatic groups, high in profile and credibility in the Manila archdiocese. World Vision provided the funding for the revision and translation of the Lumko materials. (This is an example of the Catholic-Protestant cooperation that is part of Scripture Search's larger vision.) World Vision is making the curriculum available for churches to use with their own congregations as they come to see its relevance in their own church life. The curriculum provides—as can be seen from the lesson titles—a rapid survey of the biblical story, focusing on Jesus' transformation of everyday reality:

1. On the Way to a New World (Exod. 13:17-22)
2. A World of Justice and Peace (Ps. 72:1-20)
3. The People of God Expect the King of Peace (Isa. 9:1-7)
4. The Kingdom of God Is at Hand (Matt. 4:12-22)
5. Trust Me (Matt. 8:23-27)
6. Live for Other People (Mark 3:1-6 & 3:20-21)
7. Accept Others as Brothers and Sisters (Mark 3:31-35)
8. Accept Jesus as the Son of God (Matt. 16:13-17)
9. Mary—the Mother of Our Lord (Luke 1:26-28)
10. The New Man Judges People in a New Way (Mark 12:38-44)

11. The New Man Solves Quarrels in a New Way (Matt. 5:43-48 and 7:12)
12. The New Family Lives in a New Way (Mark 10:1-9)
13. The New Man Prays in a New Way (Matt. 6:7-15)
14. The New Man Stands up for the Despised Ones (Matt. 8:1-4)
15. Jesus is Our Unshakable Hope (Matt. 5:1-10)

The model itself

Mac Bradshaw explains what is involved in moving from life to Bible as it is used in the World Vision context:

1. The place that Scripture Search fits in most naturally is in the reflection period of the action-reflection-action group-learning process. Groups meet frequently to review their actions in carrying out previous plans and to extract lessons from both the strengths and weaknesses of their experience and then to approach action again, but hopefully wiser and better skilled.

2. The project facilitator, or a member of the group, comes prepared to introduce a Scripture reading during reflection period when experience-sharing is at a high point. Preaching or teaching on the text is discouraged. The only information that is given by the facilitator is enough background material to make sure the original setting of the event is in its context. The story or verses chosen are handled like a case study in the case study method of learning.

3. It is the people themselves who discover the relevance of the case study from Scripture to their lives in light of the issues the group is wrestling with. Facilitators use a variety of methods to draw out people's insights and participation through use of questions.

4. Three fundamental questions are essential to be answered, though they may be brought out in various interesting ways.
   A. What are similarities between their experience (in the Biblical times) and our experience now? (This leads to contextualization.)

    B. What light does their experience cast upon our experience? (This leads to prayerful reflection.)

    C. What should we do about these insights as a group and personally? (This leads to actualization.) The last question forms a bridge into the new plans for group action which helps to insure that the Scriptures are lived obediently and practically. Obedience/nonobedience are accounted for in the next meeting.

5. Facilitators are finding that selection of appropriate Scripture stories is made easier if positive and negative values and attitudes emerging in the group's experience are identified. The subject matter of group reflections (self-esteem, servant leadership, etc) normally does not touch on dogma or the specifically "religious." Rather they are focused upon values encountered in everyday life.

The assumptions

Scripture Search is driven by at least three sets of assumptions that enliven and empower it. More than the specific techniques (sets of questions and so on), these assumptions may be the heart of what Scripture Search brings to our common quest to hear and respond faithfully to Scripture.

About Scripture

Scripture Search represents a fundamental reorientation in the assumptions normally found within the Western Christian tradition, within which we tend to assume:

❖ Scripture is primarily addressed to the individual.

❖ Scripture is primarily about spiritual things.

❖ Scripture is primarily about the world to come.

❖ Scripture is primarily written from the divine point of view.

The prevailing first three assumptions are part of the Enlightenment adjustment that makes a sharp demarcation between the public and private spheres, assigning reason to the public sphere and faith to the private sphere. The fourth was virtually universally accepted as self-evident until after that adjustment.

Scripture Search assumes:

- ❖ Scripture is primarily addressed to the community (and therefore to the individual-in-community).
- ❖ Scripture is about all spheres of life (and therefore also about the spiritual).
- ❖ Scripture is primarily about this world (and so, by extension, also about the world to come).
- ❖ Scripture is primarily written from the divine point of view, which is also the view from among those who are "the least of these my brethren" (Matt. 25:40).

To expand on each of these, "Scripture primarily addressed to the community" means first that all the material in both the Old Testament and New Testament regarding life in community, whether narrative, legal or hortatory, now becomes relevant. Further, it is not simply that Scripture addresses community issues, but that people hear Scripture in community, and the community holds its members responsible for their hearing of and response to Scripture.

"Scripture is about all spheres of life," and God is concerned with all spheres of our lives. Thus all of the group's decisions, whether regarding sharing of responsibilities, allocation of resources or response to a neighbor's need, become occasions for both obedience to and empowerment from the Word of God.

"Scripture is primarily about this world." Construals of the gospel that place heavy emphasis on the world to come tend to reduce salvation to a single-person guaranteed reservation in the celestial lodgings (rather than the infernal). A recovery of Scripture's focus on this world recovers a lively sense of God's passion for this world and for our neighbor. From the Scripture's point of view, the question of salvation in the world to come is not simply, "Am I saved?" but "Do I really want to spend the next life too in the presence of this God who is continually placing before me the most disquieting neighbors?"

"Scripture is primarily written from the divine point of view, which is also the view from among those who are 'the least of these my brethren'" (Matt. 25:40). That is, Scripture is as much written "from below" as "from above." This is not a statement about the importance of the human element in Scripture, although we should not undervalue that either. Rather, it is an acknowledgement that God in Scripture is more often found among the Hannahs and Marys at the fringes than in the temple. In the Philippines context, Isaiah 65:17-25 plays a key role in Scripture Search, with a text announcing, "They shall build houses and inhabit them." To feel *that* in one's gut as good news—rather than, say, as a statement of the obvious—is to tap into the rootedness of Scripture among the poor, a rootedness which Scripture Search is beginning to recover.

This shift in assumptions is easy to describe, but in fact it is an extended process. The important thing about Scripture Search is not its techniques (which are largely generic), but the opportunity it provides, over time, for groups to experience what it is to encounter Scripture as these assumptions begin to shift.

About the project community

Mac Bradshaw believes there are several assumptions in World Vision's view of the ministry of transformation and the work of God in community life in its use of Scripture Search as a method:

1. God is already at work in a community before we even come on the scene.
2. The members of a community have accumulated a great deal of wisdom about a variety of topics including spiritual perspectives on life.

3. The method emphasizes the absolute necessity of the community taking responsibility for its own spiritual pilgrimage rather than simply adopting a pre-planned one from elsewhere.

4. People in community are capable of making their own application of spiritual truth in their local situation.

5. Scripture Search method recognizes that World Vision's presence in a community through a project is not the sole source of Christian nurture in the community. The local churches present have a major responsibility for contributing to the spiritual nurture of their members, hence Scripture Search is non-pros-elytizing.

About World Vision's role

And what is World Vision's role in the process? According to Bradshaw: "World Vision's charism is probably more that of people discovering the King by gradual acquaintance of His ways through experiencing His reign in specific issues/problems of living, the experience being interpreted by their own search of an appropriate Scripture case alongside their experience. Other charisms, such as that of evangelistic outreaches, are more fitting to overt 'church growth' than is the development process."

For each of these sets of assumptions, the importance of Scripture Search is that it provides a space for the community to work out these assumptions.

What Are the Results of Scripture Search?

Individuals are changed . . .

❖ One core group member describes the effects of Scripture Search: "It's meant a change from just reading the words to understanding and meditating on the Word of God. I've gone from reading comics to reading the Bible. I'm seeing the Lord provide for family needs. Before, my world was limited to dressmaking and household chores; now I'm also trying to aid the community around me. I've learned to have 'heart to heart' talks with the Lord."

❖ Another core group member said: "I didn't want to listen to anyone. What do they have to say to me? I was very proud. But one time we read the story about Jesus and the woman at the well. Jesus listened to that woman. If Jesus listened to that woman, maybe I should listen to the others in the group. 'Have this mind in you which was also in Jesus Christ.' Jesus humbled himself; I should too."

❖ Scripture Search has had a marked impact on the husband of another of the core group leaders. At the start, while drunk he would stare across the yard at the group engaged in its study. Shortly after the studies started, he stopped drinking. He asked that someone read the Bible loud enough so that he could hear too. He is now taking the initiative in getting the family to church. He is even reading Scripture himself, although surreptitiously.

❖ It should not, perhaps, have been surprising that those first affected by Scripture Search were the facilitators themselves. One facilitator was personally challenged and, choosing to interpret this challenge as coming from colleagues, decided to leave. Another facilitator found her definition of an acceptable husband radically changed.

Groups are changed (planning) . . .

In doing project planning, one recurring question is whether to start with a realistic assessment of resources or with the immediate needs. In these contexts, Scripture Search turns to Jesus' example, which tends to open up the options the core group considers.

❖ A group beginning to plan reflected on the creation story of Genesis 1. The group reflected by drawing pictures, and then discussing their drawings. The drawings were a way of freely exploring the text. One drawing showed an exhausted

73

swimmer, illustrating what would have happened had humans been created before dry land ("We were created after all our needs were provided for"). Another showed a human form resting in bed (God on the seventh day). "Our project work, involving planning, implementation, and evaluation," suggested the facilitator, "does have some parallels in the process Genesis 1 describes." After exploring the text the group agreed, and the process itself encouraged them to value their work more highly.

Groups are changed (setting agendas for group change) . . .

❖ One community identified alcoholism and other vices as problems. Was it, the core group wondered, because of a lack of personal relationships with the Lord? "What should we do?" asked the facilitator. The ideas came: "Let's study the Word of God" and "Let's start and end meetings with prayer." And so an explicit focus on the people's relationship with God emerged at the core group's initiative.

❖ A group beginning a project reflected on reasons for past failure, including mismanagement and misappropriation of funds for personal use. "People tend to be extravagant, spending all their money in a matter of days and having a [reckless] or fatalistic attitude toward the future." As a result, the group turned to the parable of the talents (Matt. 25:14-30) to reflect on the qualities their leaders would need if the project were to succeed this time.

❖ Another group had been engaged in Scripture Search for some months. As a result of this cumulative interaction with Scripture and each other, it occurred to them that God might not be as pleased as they were about their illegal but efficient tap into the city's power lines. In the process of regularizing their situation, more than one surprised utility company employee was given a fresh glimpse of what following Jesus might mean.

Groups are changed (interpersonal relationships) . . .

❖ One community isolated a couple because they believed one of them (the couple) was a witch. The core group discussed this at length. Finally, the facilitator insisted on going to visit the couple; the core group insisted that the facilitator have an escort of two large men carrying swords. As a result of this visit and subsequent meetings, the couple was eventually accepted and now serve as leaders in the community.

❖ In the course of one meeting, a discussion over strategy was turning into a heated dispute. "Is this how we handle disagreements?" someone asked. The ensuing discussion brought public requests for forgiveness, reconciliation and a return to the strategy discussion.

❖ At one meeting, the core group realized that a spouse's jealousy of the amount of time one of them was having to devote to group activities had become a serious problem. Another member suggested that the group reflect on 1 Corinthians 13. "What do we do about it?" The group decided to serenade the family at 4:00 a.m. (a traditional way of giving affirmation). As a result, the formerly jealous spouse is now also active in the core group, and the core group continues to acquire practice in serenading.

Issues

Scripture Search is in process, and currently wrestling with a number of issues of broad interest, including balancing Scripture Search with other methods and training (resourcing) facilitators.

Scripture Search and other methods

The issue of balancing Scripture Search with other methods relates to the necessary balance between "Bible-to-Life" and "Life-to-Bible" approaches. One way of thinking about these approaches to Scripture is to place them on an x-y axis like the one in Figure 5.1 on page 76.

"Low accountability" would be characteristic of most situations in which Scripture is taught in large group settings; "high accountability" is characteristic of most small group settings. "Bible-to-Life" is used for approaches that stress hearing what questions extended portions of Scripture wish to place before us; "Life-to-Bible" is for those that stress exploring how Scripture might respond to questions we bring to it. Scripture Search would fall more or less where the "SS" appears in Figure 5.1.

Note that in this grid the horizontal and vertical axes are not symmetrical. It would be worth reflecting—somewhere else—whether "low accountability" encounters with Scripture are desirable. It is clear that many "low accountability" encounters are not. On the other hand, it is fairly clear that "Bible-to-Life" and "Life-to-Bible" approaches need each other. A group can probably begin with either approach, but neither can remain healthy for very long if its counterpart is weak.

In practical terms, this means that World Vision is properly concerned that there are adequate "Bible-to-Life" approaches present where it is promoting Scripture Search.

Figure 5.1: "Bible-to-Life" and "Life-to-Bible" Approaches

High
accountability

SS

Bible to Life ←——————————→ Life to Bible

Low
accountability

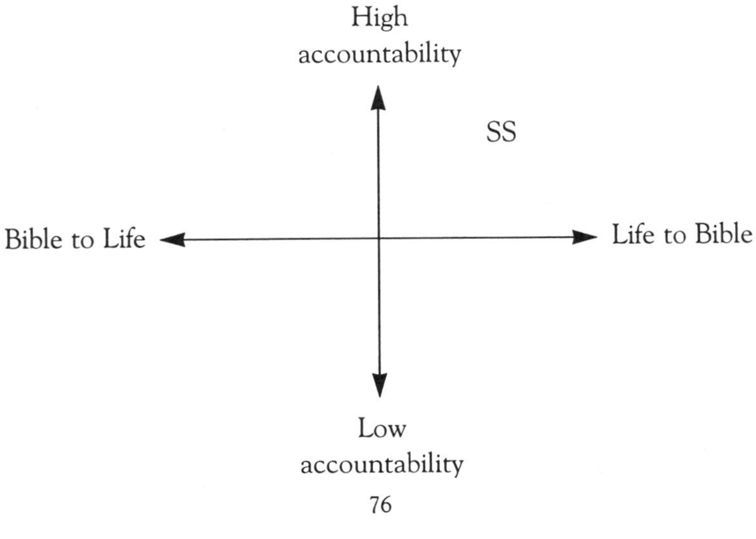

World Vision recognizes—surely defensibly—that such "Bible-to-Life" approaches are more properly the bailiwick of local congregations. But World Vision cannot successfully encourage Scripture Search where these approaches are weak (or absent).

Training

Training (and providing ongoing resources) for facilitators involves a number of issues. First, facilitators need a set of general facilitation skills, whatever the subject matter may be.

Second, familiarity with Scripture is necessary for Scripture Search to work. At its most practical, it comes down to the question of what text to use for the next meeting. In response to this need, facilitators are trading their growing lists of texts that have worked well in connection with particular topics with one another. Further, staff members and national advisors are recommending various helps (concordances, chain reference Bibles, *The Serendipity Bible* and so on).

While it is true that these latter measures are in part stop-gap, and that they in part reflect gaps in the formation of the facilitators, a more important truth is that Scripture Search is placing fresh demands on the church, calling it to hear and respond to Scripture in new ways. So to an important degree the lists of texts that the facilitators are trading with each other, along with their accompanying experiences and insights, reflect the cutting edge of the church's hearing and responding to Scripture in that time and place.

The third training issue is more pastoral: Since Scripture Search appears to challenge first the facilitators themselves to transformation, what sorts of pastoral support do they need so that this will be a creative, instead of a destructive, experience?

The fourth training issue relates to the need to move Scripture Search beyond the core group and the planning groups and into the warp and woof of the community itself. Here the challenge is to keep the previous issues from becoming too much of a bottleneck. The practical issue at this point is the need for materials in Tagalog and other languages and dialects.

The last training issue is that of non-text-based approaches. World Vision facilitators are experimenting in various ways with non-text-based aids to discussion, including drawing and role-playing. (This is an area that could profit from further exploration, e.g., audio cassettes?)

Conclusion

Scripture Search is one of the most hopeful approximations within the experience of World Vision to an integration of Scripture in ministry. Not only is it a question of expanding the horizons against which Scripture is read (from individual, other-worldly, spiritual to community, this-worldly, all dimensions), it integrates community development, spiritual nurture and evangelism in one activity. Where Scripture Search is in place, there is a reduction of the dangers of a disembodied gospel and a one-dimensional development.

As argued earlier, Scripture Search is driven by at least three sets of assumptions that enliven and empower it. More than the specific techniques (sets of questions, and so on), these assumptions may be the heart of what Scripture Search brings to our common quest to hear and respond faithfully to Scripture.

As argued, Scripture Search needs, for its own health, a correspondingly strong program of "Bible-to-Life" study rooted in the local churches and their members. At the same time, it would be a mistake to insist too strongly on one particular way of doing this. In this regard, it is encouraging that the Lumko series appears to be treated as exemplary, rather than normative.

NOTES

1   In this chapter only, I use "World Vision" or "World Vision in the Philippines" interchangeably. All other references to World

Vision that appear in this book refer to the international World Vision Partnership, unless otherwise noted.

2   The cycle of action-reflection (or action-reflection-action) is used by some Christian and non-Christian groups working in community development and is inspired by the work of Paulo Freire. Its primary insight is that group learning needs to come from reflection on the group's first-hand experience, and that this reflection needs to influence subsequent actions by the group.

3   Quotations and excerpts attributed to Malcolm (Mac) Bradshaw are taken from two in-house documents that he wrote for World Vision in the Philippines.

6

The Models from
Transformation

To establish a broader context for the models presented in chapters 2-5, I now offer brief descriptions of the models presented between 1985 and 1993 in the series "Wholistic models of evangelism and social concern" in *Transformation*, and identify dimensions of ministry present in these and the models of chapters 2-5.

AMEXTRA

Mexico contains the world's largest city, Mexico City, which rushes headlong into the twenty-first century. It also contains around 120,000 small communities of less than 3,000 people, for whom the twentieth century is largely a matter of hearsay. Sergio Sanchez, the director of AMEXTRA, originally comes from one of these small communities. His experiences in both the small community and in Mexico City, informed by dialogue with groups like the International Fellowship of Evangelical Students and the Latin American Theological Fraternity, found expression in the creation of AMEXTRA.

AMEXTRA, the Mexican Association for Rural and Urban Transformation, defines its task in this way: "To facilitate processes of change and wholistic transformation in people, families, and communities so that they may improve their quality of living and have hope for a better and fruitful life."

While not losing a concern for the individual before God, AMEXTRA is learning to understand and express this within a larger concern for God's will for the individual in community. AMEXTRA works with both communities and churches to promote initiatives in areas such as primary health care, agricultural techniques, job skills training and small business development. This work is channeled through Communal Transformation Programs (cooperating with local churches and regional parachurch groups), Ecclesiastical Programs of Service (local churches), and Volunteers Action Programs (individual volunteers, Christian and non-Christian). Currently AMEXTRA is working in the regions of Chiapas, Oaxaca, Ajusco, Yucatan, Puebla, Chalco Valley and the state of Mexico.

When asked about their motivation for these activities, AMEXTRA talks of God as Creator and our responsibility of stewardship. "A woman in a rural meeting told us that she sees God behind our services and that He was the only one who can encourage us to do it."

John Bosco

Robin Paul, the development coordinator for the Methodist Church in Karnataka, India, narrates what happened when a committed Christian started as a management trainee in an Indian factory in 1977. Things began well for John Bosco, until he noticed how management treated the workers. Against the advice of colleagues ("John, the workers are third-rate people! Why do you bother about them?"),[1] John began working to establish a union. In time he became a union leader. A dream he had "in which Jesus carrying a cross was staring at John and the workers," confirmed John's course.

Faced with management opposition, John turned to Scripture (Ps. 53.4-5):

> *Have those who work evil no understanding,*
>> *who eat up my people as they eat bread,*
>> *and do not call upon God?*
> *There they are, in great terror,*
>> *in terror such as has not been!*
> *For God will scatter the bones of the ungodly;*
>> *they will be put to shame, for God has rejected them.*

God was speaking. That was certainly very clear to John that early morning. He was telling him He was involved (verse 5). They [the management] were in great fear where no fear had been, this was his answer. How God was going to instill fear into the management John did not know. But one thing he knew was that God was with him and involved and that he was urging him to press on.

The workers got their union. But management did not forgive John, and dismissed him in 1983. Robin Paul recounts:

> Along with some of those who resigned he decided to start a similar industry as the Light Company employing handicapped people to show the company how a company can run with proper labour practices and with Christian principles.

> As a direct result of this activity in the factory over these years a church was planted. Most of the workers and their families lived in a slum immediately across the road from the factory. The inhabitants included both Hindus and Moslems. As the people saw the way John Bosco and his Christian colleagues and friends were involved with their problems, the worst drunkards in the factory, other workers and some residents of the slum all became Christians. A small room was set aside in the slum for a Christian worship hall and for educating and training workers and

their families in various skills. The people summed up their response by saying, "By what you have done you have painted us a portrait of Jesus."

Within the collection of models, this one is noteworthy, first, because of its unintentional nature. John did not plan either the union activity or the church planting. It is also noteworthy for its mixture of advances and setbacks.

Douglas Hall

In the minds of many, "Boston" brings to mind white Anglo-Saxon Protestants, past and present. But Boston has traditionally also been a center for other ethnic groups, notably the Irish, and more recently blacks from the southern United States and Hispanics. Douglas Hall, serving as executive director of the Emmanuel Gospel Center in Boston, a center dedicated to the long-term development of urban churches and communities, writes from his experience with these ethnic groups.

Citing examples from a variety of local ministries, Hall contrasts a product orientation and a process orientation and advocates the latter. The product orientation is widespread in management literature, both secular and Christian. It analyzes the problem, forms an objective, defines goals to meet the objective, outlines a strategy to meet the goals, employs tactics to advance the strategy, reviews the results, determines which review may contribute to a further analysis of the problem and so on.

This process appears self-evident to many. Hall has seen a very different process at work in some Boston churches, and attempts to describe it, calling it "the relational process." It is a process of observation, positive appreciation, communication, meeting perceived needs, meeting basic needs and multiplication.

Hall sees the process at work in the Bible:

Observation: God observes people and events on earth. We find him observing Adam and Eve. . . . The Bible says he even watches the sparrow.

Positive appreciation: God so loved the world that he gave. He is described as a loving God who longs to gather us under his wings as a mother bird gathers her chicks. . . .
Communication: God desires two-way, intimate communication with us. . . . Jesus was so effective as a communicator that the religious people wanted to kill him and the common people mobbed him so that at times he could not move about freely.
Meeting perceived needs: Jesus spent hours healing the sick and delivering people from evil spirits. He was always conscious of how people understood their own needs. . . .
Meet basic need: Though we did not know it, our most basic need was for salvation. Jesus met this through the cross and his resurrection. . . .
Long-term multiplication: Jesus prepared his leaving so that more would be accomplished after he left than was accomplished while he was here.

In the South End Neighborhood Church (the church that the Halls attend and that appears to have shaped Hall's vision), there are a significant number of recovering addicts and alcoholics, not because there are specific programs, but because "they feel they can belong there." Or, because "the church followed a process of observation, positive appreciation, communication, meeting perceived needs, meeting basic needs, and multiplication."

Generalizing, Hall argues:

Churches in Boston meet the types of needs that agencies and parachurch organizations meet in other places. For example, we do not have Christian prison halfway houses here, but 90 percent of the parishioners of at least one church have prison records. We do not have the number of Christian drug programmes here that we need, but we have churches in which most of the congregation are recovering addicts and alcoholics. . . . Churches are sponsoring food pantries, prison outreach, and a variety of social programmes. Many of these programmes have started spontaneously as churches find ways to meet the needs of their members and neighbours.

In these examples the strongly relational nature of the process orientation becomes clear. As a result, Hall can report impressive church growth among immigrants, citing, in particular, Brazilian, Haitian and Hispanic groups. Among these groups it is expected that the pastor will involve himself in the full range of the parishioners' problems. This is bolstered by the pragmatics of the situation: "The church planter who plants a church in a poor area only gets paid when the people 'make it' both socially and spiritually. So he is naturally involved in both social responsibility and evangelism."

Holistic Ministries International

Waldron Scott, president of Holistic Ministries International (HMI), begins his description of the organization with a description of its context:

> Paterson [New Jersey] is very much a Two-Thirds World city: densely populated, ethnically diverse, economically impoverished. . . . Founded by Alexander Hamilton in 1792 as America's first planned industrial city . . . . Many of its families are on welfare; even more are headed by single parents. . . . The people are proud of their history. One of America's premier 20th-century poets, William Carlos Williams, produced an epic poem titled *Paterson*. The city has upwards of 200 churches, many of them store-fronts, and a number of active neighbourhood associations.

Waldron and Georgia Scott have been shaped by and have helped to shape the Plymouth Brethren, the Navigators, the World Evangelical Fellowship and the American Leprosy Mission. They moved to Paterson in 1984 and founded HMI "to develop a set of ministries that would manifest, in word and deed, the good news of the Kingdom of God; and to develop a context in which prospective missionaries, from Paterson and elsewhere, might receive training relevant to twenty-first century mission."

They came without a plan for carrying out the vision, and spent time getting to know the city. They joined a local church, Madison Avenue Christian Reformed Church, "a small, racially integrated, inner city congregation." Eventually they started Loving Care, an early learning center for pre-schoolers. One parent who used the center was a key city official, contact with whom led to involvement in Leadership Paterson, a program for equipping citizens for civic engagement. The time the Scotts have devoted to civic life reflects their understanding of the fish aphorism.

> We have all heard the aphorism, "If you give a man a fish you feed him for a day; but if you train him how to fish you feed him for a lifetime." This is true as far as it goes but it overlooks two equally essential issues: it does not help a man to learn how to fish if he is denied access to the stream; and it may even kill him if the stream is polluted. We are trying to work simultaneously on all four levels: charity, training, access and accountability.

Understanding the anatomy of the city and meeting its decision-makers relates directly to both halves of the HMI vision: manifesting the good news of the kingdom and providing training relevant for twenty-first century mission.

Opportunities for ministry have continued to appear. Together with the Navigators, HMI co-sponsors an English as a Second Language program for new Hispanic immigrants. At the time of this writing, Georgia Scott chaired the Citizens' Alliance for a Drug-Free Paterson. Developing these ministry opportunities into training opportunities is a task for the future.

Living Word Community

Ronald Klaus, a leader in the Living Word Community—

a multi-ethnic and bilingual church in urban Philadelphia, U.S.A.—describes the community and its background. Klaus traces the church's history, which is rooted in the Welsh Revival of 1904, the Pentecostal movement and the founding of the Philadelphia Gospel Temple. In the 1960s the congregation's leadership, concerned about preserving the fruits of revival, restructured congregational life around three goals: spirituality, community and mission. Klaus recounts: "All centralized activities except the Sunday morning worship service were canceled. Even Sunday School was eliminated! The life of the congregation was radically decentralized around several small home meetings."

The result of these changes was "explosive" growth, with the creation, through intentional division, of additional congregations. Because of these divisions, the congregation in the center city was now "a truly urban congregation . . . For the first time we would be drawn into the problems that urban churches face."

Blacks, Hispanics and Anglos found themselves together in the congregation, and life together required attention:

> Our home-meeting-centered and discipleship-based model of church life now became even more important to our very heterogeneous congregation. Racial and ethnic differences have at times produced a great deal of tension among us. However, the home meetings gave us a forum in which to talk these differences out. . . . We see this kind of modeling of relationships and love across societal boundaries to be a crucial foundation to our social outreach.

In 1982 the congregation engaged in an extensive evangelistic effort, with the greatest response in Hispanic North Philadelphia. Follow-up meant commitment to this area, with members of the Center City congregation relocating or learning Spanish. In 1987 a new bilingual congregation was launched—

the North Philadelphia Congregation of the Living Word Community. Ministry consists mainly of being in the community and establishing relationships with the local residents: "We try to love them where they are and minister to them according to their particular needs." Ministry embraces evangelism in a variety of forms. It also embraces social action (e.g., in coordination with HACE, the Hispanic Association of Contractors and Entrepreneurs) and prayer for God's miraculous intervention:

> A theology that emphasizes God's immanence and his willingness at times to act miraculously has been a distinct asset. The miraculous answers to prayer which we have seen in such areas as physical healing bring a great sense of hope to people who don't have time to wait until the "system" solves their problems.

Within the *Transformation* series, this study is noteworthy for showing how the congregation developed over time, and how growth in one area opens possibilities for growth in others.

Diocese of Mt. Kenya East

Northeastern Kenya encompasses both the semi-deserts in the north, which are home to nomadic groups, and the fertile and densely-populated south. The Anglican Diocese of Mt. Kenya East has the challenge of serving both areas. Priorities, identified locally, include "pastoral care, evangelism and teaching; health, agriculture and social welfare; education, industry, road building and construction."

When she wrote about the Diocese, Grace Wanjiru Gitari was the diocesan chairperson of the Mothers' Union in the Diocese of Mount Kenya East (Anglican). She describes the diocesan vision of Christian mission that underlies these activities.

"We have adopted," she writes, "a slogan to explain our work: 'And Jesus increased in wisdom and in stature, and in favor with God and man' (Luke 2:52)."

In this verse we find four aspects of development which are just as necessary in the life of a community as they were in the individual human development of our Lord:

- ❖ Wisdom, or mental and intellectual development;
- ❖ Stature, or physical development;
- ❖ "In favor with God . . ."; spiritual development;
- ❖ ". . . And man"; social development.

With regard to "wisdom," the Diocese both sponsors primary and secondary schools and provides a variety of consultancy services to other schools. The Diocese has created the Christian Industrial Training Centre, providing training in trades such as carpentry, masonry and dressmaking. Addressing diocesan needs, the St. Andrew's Institute for Mission and Evangelism trains clergy, community health workers, lay evangelists, typists, radio broadcasters and writers.

As for "stature," programs focus on food, clothing and shelter. Community health workers teach nutrition. A rural development program focuses on livestock development and water-catchment in the semi-desert areas. The Mothers' Union provides resources for mothers in the communities, a key link in any sustainable development. The focus on shelter includes shelter for clergy at retirement, for which purpose the Diocese created a cooperative (loan) society.

"In favor with God" implies the foci of evangelism and discipling. How does one do evangelism among nomads? The Diocese gave one pastor a camel with which to follow his congregation. Other evangelists were entrusted with the diocesan goats, "and sent out to mingle with their fellow pastoralists, preaching the gospel as they went." Whether in rural or urban areas, effective teaching remains a priority.

"In favor with man" implies a variety of initiatives, including the work of the social welfare department, the community development officers and the Mothers' Union. The latter "concentrates on the work of the family in all its aspects, in the belief that the family is the pillar of all human life."

Finally, while the Diocese recognizes the need for specialization and specialized training, it emphasizes the need for integration. Thus "the parish evangelist may be a community health worker. The Diocesan architect visits secondary schools to preach to the students. Jesus needed to experience all four kinds of growth, and so too do we."

Our Lady's Youth Center

The story of Our Lady's Youth Center in El Paso, Texas, is described by Paul Leavenworth of Biola University in La Mirada, California. Father Rick Thomas arrived at the Center in 1964. He built "a well organized and efficient program," but wanted more. In 1969 he and the Center encountered the charismatic renewal. The defining moment for the Center came in 1972. Members of a prayer group from the Center had read Luke 14:12-14 ("When you give a dinner or a banquet, do not invite your friends or your brothers . . .). They decided that God was calling them to celebrate Christmas dinner with the residents of the garbage dump in Juarez, Mexico. They went to the dump, negotiated a truce between the dump's factions, and served the dinner. Only later did they realize that they had served twice the number of dinners they had brought.

Since that moment, the Center has become the hub of a set of programs oriented toward the poor in El Paso and Juarez. Programs include "The Lord's Food Bank, The Lord's Ranch, the independently operated [Cooperative Association of Materials Handlers] . . . The Lord's Medical Clinic, La Cueva Counseling Center, Los Jardines de Dios Orphanage, Tepeyac Federal Credit Union, and prison and hospital visitation."

Because of the truce established in 1972, the leaders of the garbage dump factions formed the Cooperative Association of Materials Handlers. It "provides a means to sell the articles gleaned from the dump, and payment of workers in proportion to the work that they have done. It also provides educational, medical, and emergency welfare resources for its members."

Summarizing, Leavenworth writes: "Evangelism, healing and social action seem to flow from the same source. The simple obedience of a few faithful people has resulted in a most amazing outpouring of God's compassion upon the poor."

John Perkins

Stephen Berk, a history professor at California State University, Long Beach, relates John Perkins' experience and the ministries Perkins has created. As Berk notes, Perkins' experience is intimately and intentionally related to the larger social issue of blacks in North America.

Perkins was born and raised in Mississippi, and sent to California by his family after a white police officer killed his brother. Perkins found Christ in California, and began ministering in youth work camps. He kept encountering young blacks from the South in the U.S.. He decided to return, "to identify with my people there, to help them break out of the cycle of despair . . . by showing them new life right where they were."

Perkins returned to Mississippi in 1960 with no particular plan in mind. "I don't like to define anything too tightly before it works. That's how you kill things." Locating in Mendenhall, Mississippi, by the mid-sixties his Voice of Calvary ministries had established a Bible institute, adult vocational classes, a day care center and the local headstart program. He began experimenting with cooperatives, which resulted in agricultural, food, housing, medical and retail co-ops. As the U.S. civil rights movement gained steam, Voice of Calvary headed the local voter registration drive. In 1969, Perkins led a boycott of the local white retail businesses, and was beaten, almost to death, by the Mississippi Highway Patrol.

Berk describes the transformation the beating brought:

While being battered he [Perkins] had become aware of the wildly contorted expressions on the faces of his assailants, so twisted were they by their hatred. Even while enduring this massive assault, Perkins had begun to see that these deranged whites were also victims of the system of evil, in bondage to their hatred.

From then on, racial reconciliation would be a part of Voice of Calvary and Perkins' agenda. Thus, for example, Voice of Calvary's church in Jackson, Mississippi, has a congregation "almost equally black and white" and corresponding leadership.

Perkins moved to Pasadena, California, in 1981 and established the Harambee Christian Family Center, focusing on spiritual nurture and vocational training. He has worked to interpret the black struggle to white audiences and to challenge affluent Christians to respond via "relocation, reconciliation, and redistribution."

Servants to Asia's Urban Poor

An outgrowth of the charismatic movement in New Zealand, Servants to Asia's Urban Poor works incarnationally in a number of Asian cities, including Bangkok and Manila. Michael Duncan is a leader of Servants' Philippine team, and wrote about the organization for *Transformation*.

Servants understands that incarnation implies that a ministry team reside in the slum itself. This is not understood as a question of effectiveness, but as a question of obedience and solidarity.

Early Servants teams involved themselves in a wide range of mercy ministries, evangelism and, subsequently, power encounters that sought the manifestation of God's power over demons, sickness and sin. This phase ended surprisingly:

The poor asked us to stop our mercy ministries, especially the loan scheme that was enabling many to start micro income-generating projects. They argued that much of

what we were doing for them was in fact causing relational and communal breakdown. In other words, the
social effect of all our programme was proving harmful.

Duncan does not make the point, but one wonders
whether incarnation did not play an important role in making
it possible for the poor to speak and be heard concerning this
situation. As a result of the above incident, Servants reoriented
its efforts to the community as a whole, and to drawing on its
resources. "It was time to do mission with the poor and not so
much for the poor."

Reflecting on holism, Duncan notes that it "has demanded
of us the courage to become a people that we have never really
been before." Duncan fleshes this out in four areas. First, holism
demands being theologians as well as practitioners, moving past
being "people with jittery minds and hyperactive bodies" and
past solely devotional study of Scripture. Second, holism
demands allowing the Spirit to challenge us in other than "spiritual" things: the Spirit may also know something about development or community empowerment. Third, holism demands
being ecumenical, both continuing to affirm what is good in
one's own tradition and learning from what God has taught
other traditions. Fourth, holism demands a deeper experience of
community. "We unashamedly need each other if we are to be in
this work for the long haul."

Spreydon Baptist Church

Spreydon is a working class suburb of Christchurch, New
Zealand, the kind of suburb most pastors would stay in only
until something more prestigious came along. Murray Robertson came to Spreydon Baptist Church as the pastor more than
20 years ago and recounts their experience.

The Robertsons started with a congregation of 50. Two of
Murray Robertson's commitments were to teaching and evangelism.

I feel my primary calling as a pastor is to teach the Word
of God in a way that helps people make sense of life. So I
am committed to the systematic exposition of books of
the Bible. I'm not sure how else you can sustain a ministry
for a very long period in one place.

Robertson started visiting the homes of non-Christians
weekly, and in time the church had teams visiting every week.
Seven years after the Robertsons arrived, nearly 300 were worshiping at the church weekly.

The church entered a new phase with a visit from David
Watson, a leader in the Anglican charismatic movement in
England. Robertson and others had seen remarkable move-
ments of the Spirit, but were not sure how to introduce these
into church life. How could they avoid becoming "the next sta-
tistic in the list of charismatic disasters"? Watson's account of
the integration of the charismatic into English Anglican
churches encouraged Robertson to try this locally.

With a framework of biblical teaching we began to see our
worshiping life renewed. Prophetic gifts began to be exer-
cised. We started praying with sick people and saw some
of them healed—and the church didn't fall apart!

Simultaneously, inspired by Roland Allen's *The Sponta-
neous Expansion of the Church*, the Spreydon church began
decentralizing into several home groups.

A third phase—response to "the cry of the poor"—began
as the church sought, unsuccessfully, a site for a bigger building.

We began to wonder if we were being shown something.
Out of heart-searching and prayer came the conviction
that we should solve our space problem by starting neigh-
bourhood congregations on Sunday mornings, based on
clusters of our existing home groups. . . . The congregations have kept us in touch with the grass roots of com-

munity life. And the total church gives us the resources for effective mission.

Better hearing and responding to this cry has involved a community help center, a kingdom bank, and the formation of Servants to Asia's Urban Poor. These responses recycle back into the church's life. As Robertson puts it, "You cannot comfortably live with your best people living in squatter communities overseas while carrying on with business as usual at home."

Te Atatu Bible Chapel

The Te Atatu Bible Chapel, a multi-cultural Open Brethren assembly in Auckland, New Zealand, is described by Brian Hathaway, the church's pastor. In 1979 the church's elders decided "to permit all the gifts of the Spirit to function within the fellowship." In the following eight years membership grew from 90 to over 650 adults and teenagers as people came to faith and engaged in a variety of mission activities. "Our desire," says Hathaway, "is to take the life and power of the Holy Spirit outside the four walls of our church fellowship and into our community." Thus the Chapel's activities include:

> **Between the Banks Trust.** A community trust operated by Te Atatu Bible Chapel for the main purpose of ministering to the community. Any finance made by the trust must be used in the community. No trust money goes to the church but church money can flow to the trust. The trust also operates as a financial base with people gifting and lending money to it for development projects and loans to other Christians; most loans are interest-free.
>
> **Family Care Centre.** A centre developing to meet holistically the needs of people, using a medical practice as an initial contact point. Volunteer Christian people are available to work with medical practitioners to meet deeper, causative problems in people as the medical practitioner often has neither time nor skills to meet needs such as

marriage counselling, depression, budgeting, deep emotional hurts, grief, practical support, family counselling, terminal illness, demonization, single parent needs, or young mothers' support.

4221 Trust. Ministry touching "street kids," alcoholics and drug addicts, using family homes and farms as rehabilitation centres. Christian love and care is blended with prayer, the ministry of the Holy Spirit, and work with animals and horticulture.

These activities reflect not only the activity of the Spirit, but also the influence of the Scripture with its focus on the kingdom.

> Such an involvement within the community has meant a radical reassessment of our congregational activities and a recognition of the fact that our highest priority is to "seek first the Kingdom of God and his righteousness" in all areas of our lives. . . . We are trying to set all our church goals in terms of the Kingdom of God and recognize that the church is not an end in itself but a means to an end— the end being the establishment of the Kingdom rule of God in all areas of the life of our community.

This *kenosis* (self-emptying) of the church goes a step further: the leadership does not attempt to control these ministries:

> They do not seek to direct or govern these ministries any more than they would a person within the congregation who runs his own business in the secular field. Thus people are encouraged to seek the Lord for their own ministry's direction, to develop their own gifts and abilities, and seek God for their financial needs.

It is precisely this *kenosis* that gives reason to believe that it is the Spirit of Jesus at work in Te Atatu.

Truth and Liberation Concern

Morris Stuart, a West Indian and one of the community's leaders, describes Truth and Liberation Concern, a Christian Community in Melbourne, Australia. Truth and Liberation Concern began circa 1970 and has grown to approximately 700 members.

> As a Christian community, we seek to take "incarnation" seriously by being culturally accessible to our contemporaries [with particular concern for the poor and younger "street people"], whom we believe should not have to cross the "church culture" barrier in order to find faith in Christ. . . . We attempt to be a prophetic and radical alternative to the darkness of our Australian context, by the way we live, teach and preach the Gospel of the Kingdom. We believe that, by teaching the gospel to the community, people come to understand at what points its faith and practice diverge from the Australian culture, and at what points there is convergence, affirmation and identity with it.

That the Truth and Liberation Concern community formed from socially diverse groups is important. "Whenever the church demonstrates in its fellowship that the barriers of race, class, culture, politics, money and status have been overcome, the 'world' and the 'principalities' and 'powers' are sent a strong signal that they are losing their grip on men and their affairs." A cell-group structure nourishes community. For Truth and Liberation, "community-in-liberation from the powers" implies a continued search for appropriate forms of leadership ("servant leadership"). It also means that within this community, neither traditionally Pentecostal nor charismatic, a range of gifts (including "glossolalia, prophetic utterances and preaching, prayer for healing of the sick and weak") play a role.

The community's understanding of the kingdom of God orients both their inward and outward journeys: "The work of salvation, which is the work of building the Kingdom, is the complete restoration of all things." Service is the meeting point between the community and the wider community. "All else flows through this, [whether it be] evangelism, caring, compassion, or social and political involvement, etc." Structured ministry and mission areas include crisis counseling, marriage and family counselling, teaching, emergency accommodation, a coffee shop, a single-parent support group, a theological studies program and "world concern."

Conclusion

An itinerary to visit these ministries would cover the globe: Australia, Colombia, India, Kenya, the United Kingdom and the United States. Within the United States, the ministries range from the East Coast to the deep South, from the Texas-Mexico border to Southern California.

The set of ministries is the sort that reminds us of the power of one of the classic lists of the marks of the church: one, holy, catholic and apostolic. It is the sort that reminds us of the enduring truth of Origen's vision:

> [The poor are said to be] the rag, tag and bobtail of humanity. But Jesus does not leave them that way. Out of material you would have thrown away as useless, he fashions [people of strength], giving them back their self-respect, enabling them to stand on their feet and look God in the eye. They were cowed, cringing, broken things. But the Son has set them free!

NOTES

1   All quotations and excerpts in this chapter are taken from their respective articles in *Transformation*. Please see the bibliography for further details.

7

Dimensions of
Holistic Mission

It would be possible to bring this book to a close here. I have described ministries in London, San Mateo, Mexico City and in rural and urban communities in the Philippines (chapters 2-5). I have recalled—too briefly—the ministries profiled in *Transformation* (chapter 6). Starting with the question, "What does holistic mission look like in practice?" I would hope that these chapters have conveyed something of the richness of the answer.

So what does holistic mission look like? People—Roger Forster, Javier Paniagua, Alfonso Navarro, Bing Abadam—"fully alive" (Ireneus' definition of the glory of God). Chapters 2-5 only partially capture their vitality, the connection between the multiple ways in which the gospel has touched them, and the many ways in which they are attempting to minister to those around them. But this is evident not only in the leaders of the various ministries! What was consistently moving was encountering quite ordinary people, often very poor, who spoke with dignity and hope.

Yet, before I end this book, it is also worth asking ourselves what we can learn from these ministries. What elements or dimensions stand out? What might the emerging shape of holistic mission be? These are the questions that will occupy the next two chapters.

To summarize our journey up to this point, Figure 7.1 below shows us what we have seen.

Figure 7.1: The combined sample of ministries

Chapter	Name	Country	Church?
	AMEXTRA	Mexico	
	John Bosco	India	
	Diocese of Mt. Kenya East	Kenya	Y
	Douglas Hall	U.S.A.	
	Holistic Ministries Int'l. (HMI)	U.S.A.	
2	Ichthus Christian Fellowship	U.K.	Y
	Living Word Community	U.S.A.	Y
3	Nazarene Center of San Mateo	Colombia	Y
	Our Lady's Youth Center	U.S.A.	
4	Parish of the Resurrection	Mexico	Y
	John Perkins	U.S.A.	
	Servants to Asia's Urban Poor	Philippines	
	Spreydon Baptist Church	New Zealand	Y
	Te Atatu Bible Chapel	New Zealand	Y
	Truth and Liberation Concern	Australia	Y
5	World Vision in the Philippines	Philippines	

The "Chapter" column lists the chapter in which the study appears; where no chapter is indicated, the ministry is included in the synopsis of models that appear in chapter six. The column on the right registers the distinction between church and parachurch ministries, referred to in the following analysis. Please note that in this analysis, I often refer to the various ministries by a shortened form of their name, e.g., "Ichthus" for "Ichthus Christian Fellowship".

The following discussion focuses on those dimensions of ministry highlighted repeatedly in the models. The result is a selective picture that leaves major areas untouched. For instance, the churches included have programs of discipleship, e.g., Ichthus' "Startrite" program or the basic curriculum that the small groups cover in the Parish of the Resurrection. Of course, because these ministry descriptions are necessarily selective, the absence of a dimension in the description does not necessarily mean that the dimension is absent in the life of that group. On the other hand, the recurrence of particular dimensions is all the more significant precisely because of the selectivity.

I group the dimensions around three questions: What is the ministry? Where does ministry happen? How does ministry happen?

What	**Where**	**How**
1. Word, work and wonder	5. Option for the poor	7. Kingdom theology
	6. Incarnation	8. Relational process
2. Evangelism		9. World mission
3. Social action		10. Small group
4. Charismatic		11. Ministry groups
		12. Leadership training
		13. Servant leadership

1. Word, Work and Wonder

Many of the ministries seek to minister through evangelism and social action, which expect obvious demonstrations of God's power: word, work and wonder. This dimension appears in seven of the eight church models and in two of the eight parachurch models. Forster, Hathaway and Robertson articulate the importance of the conscious inclusion of word, work and wonder programmatically:

> The mission of the church, under the direction and in the power of the Holy Spirit, is to evangelise with words, works and wonders, which embody proclamation, presence, and power evangelism as popularly understood. (Forster, Ichthus)

> Our desire is to take the life and power of the Holy Spirit outside the four walls of our church fellowship and into our community. Thus we encourage people to proclaim the gospel by words, deeds and signs. (Hathaway, Te Atatu)

> In the ministry of Jesus, as recorded in the Gospels, we find evangelical, charismatic and justice dimensions. Unfortunately, we have put asunder what God has joined together. (Robertson, Spreydon)

However, even those groups that share this concern will come at it differently. Forster and Hathaway understand evangelism as the integrating concept for word, work and wonder. For others, like Stuart (Truth and Liberation Concern), the integrating concept is service.

From the brief histories contained in most of the models, it appears that a variety of paths lead to the word, work and wonder synthesis. At least three paths are apparent:

❖ Groups start with word and deed, and discover wonder along the way

❖ Groups respond to the charismatic with more intentional discipleship, which leads to word and deed
❖ Groups committed to word respond to the charismatic, which leads (via decentralization) to deed

Having introduced evangelism, social action and the charismatic as a single unit, we will now look at expressions of each. What the following three sections show is that it is not simply a matter of adding traditional evangelism to traditional social action to the traditional charismatic. Each affects the others; the whole is greater than the parts.

2. Evangelism

A concern for evangelism appears in all the models. To the degree that the model is incarnational (in the sense developed below), this inclusion appears to be an important part of the dynamic. Even where ministries did not plan for evangelism, they report evangelistic effects, as in John Bosco's union activity in India:

> Most of the workers and their families lived in a slum immediately across the road from the factory. The inhabitants included both Hindus and Moslems. As the people saw the way John Bosco and his Christian colleagues and friends were involved with their problems, the worst drunkards in the factory, other workers and some residents of the slum all became Christians. A small room was set aside in the slum for a Christian worship hall and for educating and training workers and their families in various skills. The people summed up their response by saying, "By what you have done you have painted us a portrait of Jesus."

The authors of the studies that appeared in Transformation tend to devote little time to questions of method. Instead, they stress the importance of a seamless integration of evangelism in the ministry. HMI and Ichthus, for example, achieve integration by deliberately choosing the kind of personal relationships that naturally result in friendship evangelism. Where this integration of evangelism has been occurring, the perception is that "stand-alone" evangelistic programs are irrelevant or inappropriate.

> A pastor once said that now they do not need to have evangelistic campaigns in his church any more, because his church is now well-known in his community and people are coming to Bible studies (and the medical checkups) of the church in a natural way. This fulfills our aim of turning the church into a transforming community that experiences day by day the joy in the service and transforming power of the Gospel in their fellow beings and in their locality. (Sanchez, AMEXTRA)

While Ichthus, Living Word, Parish of the Resurrection, San Mateo, Spreydon and Truth and Liberation Concern use canvasing, the style of canvasing reflects their understanding of holism.

> At our first point of contact with the wider community we do not ask, "Have you heard of the four Spiritual Laws?" rather, "Is there any way in which we can serve you?" (Stuart, Truth and Liberation Concern)

Nevertheless, as the experience of Servants (Philippines) illustrates, evangelism also has its own logic, which needs to be respected even when evangelism is seamlessly integrated with other ministry elements:

> We came to see that conversion demands that people come to Christ through the categories of faith and repentance. Just as we had seen that the category of projects can create rice Christians so the category of power, by itself, can also birth superficial growth. (Duncan)

In other words, if we practice evangelism without due attention to its necessary components (e.g., repentance), putting evangelism in a holistic framework will not solve the problem. In this context, the amount of time Navarro of the Parish of the Resurrection dedicates to primary evangelism to get the components right deserves attention.

The integration of evangelism in the ministry is, also, not simply a question of integration with other ministry elements, but is in practice an expression of the life of the ministering community itself. Stuart's summary of Truth and Liberation Concern's affirmations about evangelism capture this well:

❖ Evangelism is the outflow of our experience of knowing Christ; the reflex reaction of the Christian community and the Christian disciple.

❖ Evangelism is a "body" ministry. To do it effectively, we must have a body from which it can be done, and to which new members could be added.

❖ Evangelism is a work of the Holy Spirit through the life of the Christian community.

❖ Evangelism is about being. Jesus said, "You shall be my witnesses." Not "you shall say witnessing words," or "you shall do witnessing things." Rather, "You shall be a witnessing community."

❖ Evangelism is a combination of living and telling.

3. Social Action

The social action dimension is present in all the models. A useful starting point is the fish proverb, as expanded by Waldron Scott (HMI):

We have all heard the aphorism, "If you give a man a fish you feed him for a day; but if you train him how to fish you feed him for a lifetime." This is true as far as it goes but it overlooks two equally essential issues: it does not help a man to learn how to fish if he is denied access to the stream; and it may even kill him if the stream is polluted.

Thus we can identify three types of social action:

❖ *Assistential*: Giving a man a fish
❖ *Promotional*: Teaching him how to fish
❖ *Structural*: Dealing with the fence or the chemical plant upstream

While this typology is imperfect, we can use it to show the different combinations of social action strategies used by the ministries:

Assistential + Promotional
Living Word Community, Diocese of Mt. Kenya East, Nazarene Center of San Mateo, Our Lady's Youth Center, Spreydon Baptist Church, Te Atatu Bible Chapel

Assistential + Promotional + Structural
AMEXTRA, Ichthus Christian Fellowship, Parish of the Resurrection, Servants to Asia's Urban Poor, Truth and Liberation Concern, World Vision in the Philippines, Douglas Hall, John Perkins, HMI

Structural
John Bosco

Here it is worth reminding ourselves of the selective nature of our sample, for in most parts of the world the majority of churches would fall in the "no action" or "assistential only" categories.

Duncan suggests a distinction of at least equal importance to that of the assistential-promotional-structural typology:

One of our number was awakened one night by the Holy Spirit. According to him, the Spirit kept asking him one question: "Why are you here?" Initially, it seemed an absurd question. As "Servants" we were here to do things for the poor. The Spirit replied: "No, you are also here to work with the poor." This revelation sparked a revolution.

Since then, that worker has had a part in creating over a dozen community cooperatives among the poor. All these to one degree or another have been founded, financed and managed by the poor.

There is a difference between working for the poor and working with the poor, as every young couple whose parents have "helped" (read "worked for") the couple plan their wedding knows. As a number of the ministries surveyed here are learning, key questions include *who* defines the problem, *who* determines the appropriate response and *who* evaluates the results.

4. Charismatic

The charismatic dimension appears in seven of the eight church models and in two of the eight parachurch models. The historic roots of this dimension are varied. Living Word traces its roots back to the Welsh Revival and the Pentecostal Movement. Parish of the Resurrection is rooted in traditions of Mexican spirituality. The charismatic renewal of the 1960s and 1970s has influenced many of the other models. Truth and Liberation Concern has been described as "idealistically charismatic." Even with this variety, the common testimony of these groups is that the Spirit's presence is literally the difference between life and death, and makes it possible to respond to God and to their community in new ways.

Particular spiritual gifts mediate this possibility of response, or grace; the gifts most often mentioned are healing and prophecy. Klaus (Living Word) reflects on the role of healing:

A theology that emphasizes God's immanence and his willingness at times to act miraculously has been a distinct asset. The miraculous answers to prayer which we have seen in such areas as physical healing bring a great sense of hope to people who don't have time to wait until the "system" solves their problems.

It is worth noting that none of the authors offers an exhaustive listing of the gifts of the Spirit that are at work in the model. The most extensive list appears in Stuart (Truth and Liberation Concern): "Glossolalia, prophetic utterances and preaching, prayer for healing of the sick and weak, and other appropriate manifestations of the Holy Spirit." The absence of catalogues of gifts and the absence of discussions about whether any of the gifts are to be universally expected acknowledge the freedom of the Spirit. The authors tend to focus on the ways in which the Spirit's gifts contribute to the overall ministry which the Spirit is directing (e.g., Klaus and Duncan, above). The Spirit's contribution to the overall ministry appears to be an important dimension of holism.

5. Option for the Poor

The poor occupy a privileged place in the ministry, whether in its selection, design, development or evaluation. This dimension appears in 14 of the 16 models (absent in Te Atatu and Mt. Kenya East). Robertson (Spreydon) provides a typical expression of this dimension: "I believe we have a mandate from Jesus for ministry in the poorer parts of our society."

As the studies demonstrated, a variety of factors can crystalize this option, and this may occur at different points in the development of the model. Its influence on the overall shape of the model is generally considerable. For some this option is the result of a search for a viable model of ministry. For Waldron Scott (HMI), it reflects a pilgrimage encompassing the Navigators, the World Evangelical Fellowship, and the American Leprosy Missions: "The 'real world' is the world of the poor, the powerless and the oppressed. While this is not immediately apparent in the United States, on a global scale it is irrefutable."

For AMEXTRA, it reflects the search for "ministry with a wholistic perspective." For World Vision in the Philippines, it is a question of organizational commitment.

For others the poor were simply encountered. With Parish of the Resurrection and San Mateo, the staffing needs of their denominations came into play ("Javier, can you take care of this congregation while we look for someone to do it long-term?"). With Ichthus, the starting point was determined by where the initial participants lived. With John Bosco, it was a commitment discovered in the course of pursuing other plans (a management career). Contacts in California prisons with young blacks from the South prompted John Perkins' return to Mississippi.

But for others, this option represented the realization that God was calling them to encounter the poor. In the case of Our Lady's Youth Center, it started with a prayer group's response to Luke 14:12-14. For Spreydon Baptist Church:

> By the early 1980s we were well on the road to becoming another mega church . . . Then we began to hear the Lord calling us in a new direction. It came through the cry of the poor.

> It began simply enough. We were trying to acquire property to erect a bigger church building, but found none was available. We began to wonder if we were being shown something.

Duncan's description of Servants puts this pattern in broader perspective:

> During the 1970s many churches in New Zealand experienced renewal and church growth. They came into new forms of worship, ministry and community. But after about a decade of inheriting one blessing after another some churches began to ask what it was all for. This question and an attempt to answer it really birthed Servants to Asia's Urban Poor.

We must not lose sight of the fact that in a number of the models, this dimension is not in the foreground for the crucial reason that the congregation in mission is itself poor: Living Word, Mt. Kenya East, San Mateo, Parish of the Resurrection, World Vision, the churches described by Doug Hall and the church formed through John Bosco's union work.

6. Incarnation

In the studies, the word "incarnation" is used to mean that the group does ministry from within the community. Characteristically, the commitment to incarnation results in relocation and downward social mobility. Klaus (Living Word) and Scott (HMI) reflect on this dimension:

> If there is anything that our experience of ministry among the poor has shown us, it is that this idea of "Immanuel," God in our midst, is essential if any lasting social changes are to be brought about. Furthermore, until some Christians are prepared to communicate this message through their own example, by living among the poor, by relating to them and loving them, our attempts at bringing salvation, healing, and other changes to our ghettos are bound to fall short. (Klaus, Living Word)

> Other scriptural convictions I carried with me into the Paterson [New Jersey] arena included . . . an understanding of incarnation that presumes "downward mobility," simple lifestyle, long-term commitment and a readiness to work from a position of weakness. We had arrived in Paterson penniless, and spent hours standing in line with hundreds of others to collect unemployment compensation. It seemed important to us, if we were to be used ultimately to help empower others, that we demonstrate that material powerlessness is not a decisive handicap to the people of God. (Scott, HMI)

For John Perkins, incarnation is both the pattern of his life and the pattern he recommends to others: "the three R's of community development: *relocation, reconciliation, and redistribution*." (Berk).

This dimension appears in 14 of the 16 models (absent in Our Lady's Youth Center and Te Atatu). It is, roughly, evenly split between models in which a key part of the leadership relocate (AMEXTRA, Ichthus, John Perkins, HMI, Servants, Spreydon, Truth and Liberation Concern), and those in which the community itself is to a significant degree the church of the poor (Living Word, Mt. Kenya East, San Mateo, Parish of the Resurrection, World Vision, the churches described by Doug Hall, and the church formed through John Bosco's union work).

7. Kingdom Theology

When the authors articulate the theology that has developed along with their ministries, the kingdom of God occupies a privileged place. This dimension stands out in a number of the models: Ichthus, Scott, Te Atatu and Truth and Liberation Concern.

What the kingdom of God is and, therefore, what counts as an adequate theology of the kingdom are both highly disputed questions. What do the spokespersons for the models mean by "kingdom theology"?

> We live in the overlap of the kingdom of this world and the kingdom of God. In that overlap it is our business as the people of God to seek to get as much of the kingdom of heaven into this world as possible until death is swallowed right up in victory and Jesus returns for ever. Then the New Age will be upon us completely. It is with this in view that Jesus taught us to pray in Matthew 6:10, "Your kingdom come, your will be done, on earth as it is in heaven." As someone has put it, the work of the kingdom is not so much to get people out of earth into heaven, but to get as much of heaven as possible on to the earth and into people. (Mitchell, Ichthus).

The work of salvation, which is the work of building the kingdom, is the complete restoration of all things. Everything, whatever it is, wherever it is and whenever it has been created, is encompassed within God's kingdom activity of restoration. (Stuart, Truth and Liberation Concern)

Our highest priority is to "seek first the kingdom of God and his righteousness" in all areas of our lives. Thus we are seeking to hone down our "church activities" to the basic essentials (worship, fellowship and equipping) and do these really well. . . . We are trying to set all our church goals in terms of the kingdom of God and recognize that the church is not an end in itself but a means to an end—the end being the establishment of the kingdom rule of God in all areas of the life of our community. (Hathaway, Te Atatu)

What this means for the way Kingdom and Church relate is illustrated in Figure 7.2 on page 113: the Kingdom is neither a subset of the Church (#1), nor disconnected from the Church (#2). Rather, it provides the framework within which the Church has meaning (#3).

8. Relational Process

This dimension appears in Ichthus, Living Word, Servants, Doug Hall, John Perkins and HMI. The relational dimension can be described in two ways. First, is the ministry response product-oriented or relational? Hall's description of the relational process appears in the previous chapter. His chart summarizes the two processes (see Figure 7.3 on page 114).

This emphasis on a relational process captures well the orientation of John Perkins and Scott of HMI. Perkins does not like to "kill things" by attempting to "define anything too tightly before it works" (Berk). Scott's orientation is based on the recognition that God "had preceded us to the city and was

Figure 7.2: The Kingdom and the Church

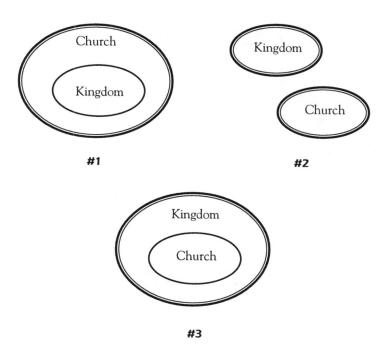

already at work in it through his people." In both cases the relational goal is to "fall in with what God was doing" (Scott).

Second, we can also describe this dimension as the contrast between meeting needs through the normal day-to-day life of the community, and meeting needs through specific programs. The former option is evident in the evolution of Ichthus' City Gates' response to the homeless in London and in Klaus' description of Living Word in Philadelphia:

> Other than the health care ministry and certain children's and young people's activities, our ministry is not highly organized or institutional. It has consisted mainly of being in the community, in some cases living there, and establishing relationships with the local residents. Outreach to

Figure 7.3: Product-oriented versus relational process

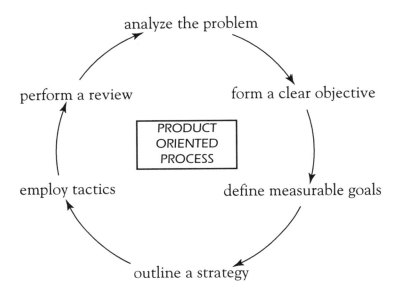

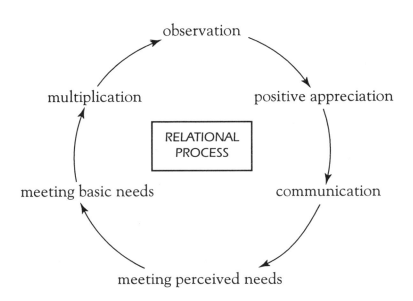

them is holistic. That is, we try to love them where they are and minister to them according to their particular needs. (Klaus)

9. World Mission

A conscious concern for world mission appears in three of the church models (Ichthus, Spreydon, Truth and Liberation Concern) and in two of the parachurch models (Servants, HMI). This concern can take many forms: partnership with Two-Thirds World Christians, support of mission societies and their missionaries, assistance to relief and development agencies or justice education in the group's own community.

Robertson's observation that "you cannot comfortably live with your best people living in squatter communities overseas while carrying on with business as usual at home" is particularly pertinent in thinking about what holism means in a concern for world mission. It is not enough that ministry extends past the parish boundaries, but rather that it affects the life of the parish itself.

10. Small Group

The strategic use of small groups appears in seven of the eight church models. Klaus explains why Living Word shifted to small groups:

> Outwardly, the congregation was growing and had all the appearances of a thriving body. The congregation had a fairly typical programme for its church life. It was highly centralized with a single pastor as the dominant leader. Meetings were large and centered around worship and teaching. Opportunities for more personalized ministry were quite limited. However, concern over spiritual vitality led to a period of intense discussion, prayer and soul-searching among the congregational leaders. During this time a number of books were quite influential, among them *The Master Plan of Evangelism* by Robert Coleman,

A Taste of New Wine by Keith Miller, *The Problem of Wine-skins* and, later, *The Community of the King* by Howard Snyder. These all pointed to the need for a different kind of church life if the fruits of revival were to be preserved.

These small groups function as the primary setting for life in community and discipling (both instruction and face-to-face accountability for the application of the instruction), and are important structures for worship and mission. They are thus not simply another possible weekly activity, but part of the core of what it means to "be church" for the membership. Does this mean that the small group meeting has become the primary expression of church life? For some, such as Te Atatu and Truth and Liberation Concern, this may be the case. More characteristically, however, the small group and the large group play complementary roles in the church's life. This is true of Parish of the Resurrection, Ichthus, Living Word, San Mateo and Spreydon.

A common discovery in the emphasis on small groups is that decentralization not only serves current goals, but also makes possible further steps in the church's development of its ministry. The small groups are not only the egg, but also the chicken.

> Our decentralized model of church life through home meetings . . . and the discipleship training model continue to be crucial factors in church life and have had a great deal to do with our eventually reaching into poor communities. (Klaus, Living Word)

> Out of heart-searching and prayer came the conviction that we should solve our space problem by starting neighbourhood congregations on Sunday mornings, based on clusters of our existing home groups. (Robertson, Spreydon)

Without the home groups as a base, the clustering and decentralization would have been less imaginable.

11. Ministry Groups

In all of the models there are groups running parallel to the small groups that are designed to respond to particular ministry needs. In some cases, the distinction between small groups and these ministry groups appears stable (e.g., Parish of the Resurrection). In other cases the dual needs of nurture and mission create a more fluid state of affairs.

> There was one other area of our life that still had not been touched by this growing mission emphasis. It was the small group ministry. . . . As we met to pray about this we had some prophetic words that the Lord was fed up with what we were doing! We were spending a great deal of time loving each other, we were told, but the Lord loved the whole world!
>
> So we called the church together, shared all this, and asked people to pray about what they thought the Lord might be saying to them about the kind of small group ministry he wanted to bring into existence. What was their dream for the kingdom? An amazing variety of answers came. It was remarkable how many had dreams of ministry with the poor and needy. (Robertson, Spreydon)

12. Leadership Training

While the leadership training dimension is predictable among the parachurch models, the surprise is that it appears in six of the church models: Ichthus, Mt. Kenya East, Parish of the Resurrection, San Mateo, Spreydon and Truth and Liberation Concern. The training component takes various forms:

> The Diocese also has training needs for its own staff. Since 1977 St. Andrew's Institute for Mission and Evangelism has become a center for training clergy, community health workers, lay evangelists, typists, radio broadcasters, writers and others. The philosophy of St. Andrew's has been to train students from all these courses side by side,

and to encourage them to mix in a single Christian community. In this way they will respect and understand one another's skills and will be able to co-operate with one another in the field. (Gitari)

One commonality is that each group realizes that education for ministry is a task they cannot afford to leave to traditional seminary education. It is not that their requirements for people to minister are more exotic, and therefore they have a larger problem than more traditional models. Rather, experiencing the same problem that the more traditional models experience, their willingness to take on new dimensions of ministry means that they have taken on this challenge also.

13. Servant Leadership

This concern is found in four of the church models (Ichthus, Spreydon, Te Atatu, Truth and Liberation Concern) and three of the parachurch models (World Vision in the Philippines, John Perkins, HMI).

> . . . the pastor's ability to see the congregation's ministry as something more than what is carried out under his supervision. (Scott, HMI)

Most of these ministries have come about as a result of the vision, commitment and development of individuals or groups of people within the congregation. The church leaders do not see their participation as one of control but one of care. Thus their role is a pastoral role and they do not seek to direct or govern these ministries any more than they would a person within the congregation who runs his own business in the secular field. . . . We have found that maximum autonomy and freedom from church governmental structures brings maximum spiritual growth within the lives of individuals involved in particular ministries and releases creative, Spirit-led vision and endeavour. (Hathaway, Te Atatu)

One of the things that has intrigued me about many charismatic groups is that having passionately affirmed their faith in the Holy Spirit, the pastor then leads with a dictatorial style! (Robertson, Spreydon)

The writer of Psalm 133 [NIV] puts it like this:
"*Behold, how good and pleasant it is*
   when brothers dwell in unity!
It is like the precious oil upon the head,
   running down upon the beard,
upon the beard of Aaron,
   running down on the collar of his robes!
It is like the dew of Hermon,
   which falls on the mountains of Zion!
For there the Lord has commanded the
         blessing,
   life for evermore."

The Lord has brought the church, the family of God, into being for two essential purposes. . . . On the one hand the church exists for nurture . . . . On the other hand, it is for mission . . . . To fulfill either function . . the church must be intact. Its foundations and its walls must be strong. The Psalmist compares "brothers dwelling in unity" with "the mountains of Zion." There must be a relationship of united brotherhood at the core of the people of God, among the leadership, if the blessing of life for evermore is to be experienced and maintained. . . .

All Biblical leadership is corporate, plural. The Godhead is corporate. Throughout history God has called individuals as leaders, but his calling has always led them into or towards a relationship of shared leadership. (Mitchell, Ichthus)

Our community also sees Jesus alone as being the head of the Church. As the head, he superintends the church through the Holy Spirit his paraclete. He apportions gifts and "offices" through this same Spirit, among which are the gifts of servant leadership (elders and bishops). . . . Government is therefore theocratic, not autocratic (by a powerful individual or group of individuals), or democratic (by the blunt instrument of the simple majority.) The style of life and government is consensus and mutual allegiance. We neither dictate nor vote, but seek together the mind of Christ for the common good." (Stuart, Truth and Liberation Concern).

The issues relating to leadership are not easy to summarize. Language like "under his supervision," "control" versus "care," "dictatorial," leadership as "corporate, plural," and "theocratic" versus "autocratic" or "democratic" is used. I have used Robert K. Greenleaf's "servant leadership" to point to this conversation.

8

The Emerging Shape
of Holistic Mission

The ministries we have looked at suggest that we are in the midst of a profound recovery of what it means to be and to act as the church. On the basis of the ministry descriptions presented in chapters 2-5, the ministries summarized in chapter six, and the analysis of dimensions of holism in chapter seven, what is the emerging shape of holistic mission? This chapter addresses this question, reshaping in a somewhat more synthetic fashion the dimensions observed in chapter seven.

The table on page 122 (see Figure 8.1) shows the relationship between the analysis in the previous chapter and this chapter's synthesis. In the column under the heading "Chapter 8," elements 1 and 6 are new, in part making explicit what is implicit in the descriptions. Elements 2, 3, 8 and 9 represent combinations of elements in the previous chapter. The remaining elements—4, 5 and 7—correspond more or less directly to elements in the previous chapter. To introduce some of these elements I use Scripture—not as proof, but to help identify what I am trying to describe or point to.

Figure 8.1: Dimensions of holism in chapters 7-8

Chapter 7	Chapter 8
What is holism?	
1 Word, work and wonder 2 Evangelism 3 Social Action 4 Charismatic	1 The church as sign of the kingdom 2 The church ministering in word, deed and sign, recovering the whole
Where is holism seen?	
5 Option for the poor 6 Incarnation	3 With the poor
How is holism expressed?	
7 Kingdom theology 8 Relational process 9 World mission 10 Small group 11 Ministry groups 12 Leadership training 13 Servant leadership	4 Through a rehearing of Scripture 5 Through an orientation of process over program 6 Through a commitment to continual conversion and learning 7 Through the local-global tension 8 Through small groups 9 Through leadership that serves this mission

Regarding the "what," this chapter also identifies in a preliminary way other conversations that can be a background resource to the conversation regarding holistic mission. It is preliminary because each of the elements has its own extensive literature. Nevertheless, the effort is worth making, for in our libraries and bookshops the tools we need are as much under the categories of "Bible" and "Theology" as they are under "Holistic Mission."

A. What is holism?

1. The church as sign of the kingdom

> *So then you are no longer strangers and sojourners, but you are fellow citizens with the saints and members of the household of God, built upon the foundation of the apostles and prophets, Christ Jesus himself being the cornerstone, in whom the whole structure is joined together and grows into a holy temple in the Lord; in whom you also are built into it for a dwelling place of God in the Spirit. (Eph. 2:19-22)*

The findings report from the Sierra Madre conference says:

> In theological discussion and reflection on practical models we felt drawn powerfully to a common vision for a kingdom community where we all live under the cross, rejoicing in the Saviour's unmerited forgiveness and knowing him as our life . . .

The first element of holistic mission is a local congregation being formed by an encounter with the one New Age that is worth talking about—the kingdom of God. This encounter is mediated by word, deed and sign (the second element), but what the first element brings into focus is that these mediations change a particular group of people so that their life together is increasingly itself good news. This element has been implicit in the descriptions. Duncan's portrait of Servants' experience captures it: "Wholism has demanded of us the courage to become a people that we have never really been before." Or again: "The work of the kingdom is not so much to get people out of earth into heaven, but to get as much of heaven as possible on to the earth and into people" (Mitchell 1986, 46). This serves as an apt description not only of Ichthus, but also of the other ministries.

The formation of something sustainable in a local congregation correlates with conversations in which Hendrikus Berk-

hof, Lesslie Newbigin, Stanley Hauerwas and William Willimon, and Gerhard Lohfink are engaged: In the day-to-day life
of the church we find the place where the powers no longer
reign (Berkhof), the place where the Spirit empowers life in
Christ (Newbigin), the place where ordinary people are
empowered to live in extraordinary ways (Hauerwas and
Willimon) and the place where we are surprised by joy
(Lohfink).

Berkhof tells us that World War II shattered his illusion
that St. Paul's "principalities and powers" could be safely
demythologized. A Dutch theologian, Berkhof has helped us
see that in cultures, institutions, multinational organizations,
public opinion and market forces we meet the principalities and
powers. We cannot live without them, but the life they support
reeks of death. Berkhof's fundamental study argues:

> All resistance and every attack against the gods of this age
> will be unfruitful, unless the church herself *is* resistance
> and attack, unless she demonstrates in her life and fel-
> lowship how men can live freed from the powers. We can
> only preach the manifold wisdom of God to Mammon if
> our life displays that we are joyfully freed from his
> clutches. To reject nationalism we must begin by no
> longer recognizing in our own bosoms any difference
> between peoples. We shall only resist social injustice and
> the disintegration of community if justice and mercy pre-
> vail in our own common life and social differences have
> lost their power to divide. (1962, 42)

In other words, "spiritual warfare" is necessary, but we will
only escape absurdity if we remember Pogo's insight: "We have
met the enemy, and he is us."

Newbigin, long-time missionary in India and now "missionary" in England, has been trying to sketch out what an
authentic missionary encounter with the First World would
look like. "The central reality," writes Newbigin, "is neither

word nor act, but the total life of a community enabled by the Spirit to live in Christ, sharing his passion and the power of his resurrection" (1989, 137). The immediate context is the classic evangelism versus social action argument. Newbigin's point is that that argument needs to be set within a broader context: "the new reality which the work of Christ has brought into being" (1989, 136).

Hauerwas and Willimon, who teach, respectively, theological ethics and Christian ministry at the Duke Divinity School (North Carolina, USA), help us understand what the church as sign of the kingdom entails from the ethical perspective. We need the church because neither our knowledge of the kingdom nor our ability to live its values are self-evident.

> The Sermon [on the Mount] implies that . . . we lack the ethical and theological resources to be faithful disciples. The Christian ethical question is not the conventional Enlightenment question, How in the world can ordinary people like us live a heroic life like that? The question is, What sort of community would be required to support an ethic of nonviolence, marital fidelity, forgiveness, and hope such as the one sketched by Jesus in the Sermon on the Mount? (1989, 80)

> We cannot say to the pregnant fifteen-year-old, "Abortion is a sin. It is your problem." Rather, it is *our* problem. We ask ourselves what sort of church we would need to be to enable an ordinary person like her to be the sort of disciple Jesus calls her to be. (1989, 80-81)

But the problem goes deeper. We do not know what the kingdom is about—an ignorance masked by our facile use of words like "justice" and "peace."

> We argue that the political task of Christians is to be the church rather than to transform the world. One reason why it is not enough to say that our first task is to make

the world better is that we Christians have no other means of accurately understanding the world and rightly interpreting the world except by way of the church. Big words like "peace" and "justice," slogans the church adopts under the presumption that, even if people do not know what "Jesus Christ is Lord" means, they will know what peace and justice means, are words awaiting content. The church really does not know what these words mean apart from the life and death of Jesus of Nazareth. After all, Pilate permitted the killing of Jesus in order to secure both peace and justice (Roman style) in Judea. It is Jesus' story that gives content to our faith, judges any institutional embodiment of our faith, and teaches us to be suspicious of any political slogan that does not need God to make itself credible. (Hauerwas and Willimon, 1989, 38)

Thus Hauerwas and Willimon argue "the political task of a Christian is to be the church rather than to transform the world" (1989, 38). It is tempting to soften this and say, "the political task of Christians is to be the church *and by this means to transform the world.*" But the problem with the softened version is that it tempts us to think that being the church is somehow straightforward. So perhaps Hauerwas and Willimon have it right.

Reflecting on public response to their book *Resident Aliens*, Hauerwas and Willimon wrote:

If ethics is the attempt to help us see the significance of the everyday and the sacredness of the ordinary, then what we attempted in the book was to help others see theologically the significance of the ordinariness of the church. We tried to show how those ordinary tasks [e.g., learning to forgive, learning how to recognize an idol] are the most determinative *political* challenge to our culture. (1991, 29)

Gerhard Lohfink, a New Testament scholar, has been deeply involved in attempting to recover community in a German Catholic context. He comes at many of these issues in his *Jesus and Community* (1984) and stresses joy.

> [In the parable of the treasure and pearl (Matt. 13:44-46),] Jesus does not say that the kingdom of God is as precious as a buried treasure or a valuable pearl. He rather compares the reign of God to two whole stories in which a poor laborer finds a buried treasure and a merchant comes upon an extremely valuable pearl. What is the decisive point of the two stories? It is neither two men's *grim efforts* to uncover a treasure or a pearl nor their *heroic separation* from their possessions. The men do give up everything and act in a radical manner, but they do so without bitterness and without heroism. They behave like men who have made a great *discovery* and have had extraordinary luck in doing so. The attraction of what they have found overwhelms them and permeates everything they do. "*Rejoicing* at his find . . ." is the decisive theme of the double parable. A profound joy, an absorption by the discovery makes it automatic for both men to sell all their possessions. They have no need to think things over first. (1984, 60)

It appears to be true that holistic ministry is a necessary response to the cry of the poor and oppressed. With Lohfink, this parable reminds us that neither the necessity nor the cry is the only starting point. He encourages us to ask, What would it mean for joy to be the starting point?

On the one hand, the work of Berkhof, Newbigin, Hauerwas and Willimon, and Lohfink underlines the importance of this lived experience of the kingdom for any paradigm of holistic ministry. On the other hand, there is a warning that we should not miss. In ministry, as in every other area, there is the temptation to focus on the "sexy" areas. Holism is "sexy," sexier than, say, learning to forgive a difficult neighbor. But without the experience of kingdom life—Hauerwas and Willimon's "ordinary"—a focus on holism is likely to be counterproductive. Thomas Merton said it best:

> Those who attempt to act and do things for others or for the world without deepening their own self-understanding, freedom and capacity to love, will have nothing to give others. They will communicate to others nothing but the contagion of their own obsessions, their aggressiveness, their ego-centered ambitions, their delusions about end and means, their doctrinaire prejudices and ideas.[1]

2. The church ministering in word, deed and sign, and recovering the whole

> *For I will not venture to speak of anything except what Christ has wrought through me to win obedience from the Gentiles, by word and deed, by the power of signs and wonders, by the power of the Holy Spirit, so that from Jerusalem and as far round as Illyricum I have fully preached the gospel of Christ.* (Rom. 15:18-19)

This point corresponds to points 1-4 in the previous chapter. It is in the context of the church as sign of the kingdom that we can affirm and celebrate the rediscovery of word, deed and sign in mission. While one of these modalities may be more evident at any given point, all three come into play as the church ministers to all those it contacts.

"Word, deed and sign" is an empirically and politically generated list. It reflects both the experience of evangelical practitioners in the post-war period and the attempts of various segments of the evangelical, Pentecostal and charismatic worlds to speak to and learn from each other. Therefore, it would be unwise to seek to ground the list non-empirically.

Nevertheless, it is worth noticing that the list dovetails with the maps Paul Hiebert, anthropologist and missiologist at Trinity Evangelical Divinity School, has been developing of various world views. Figure 8.2 below is an adaptation of Hiebert's material by Bryant Myers, World Vision International's vice president for mission and evangelism. Hiebert's insight is that the modern world view contrasts with pre-modern world views (including that reflected in the Bible) in that it makes a sharp distinction between the spiritual and physical worlds and eliminates the middle part of the spiritual-physical continuum (demonic possession, leprechauns, shamans, vampires, and so

Figure 8.2: The modern and biblical world views

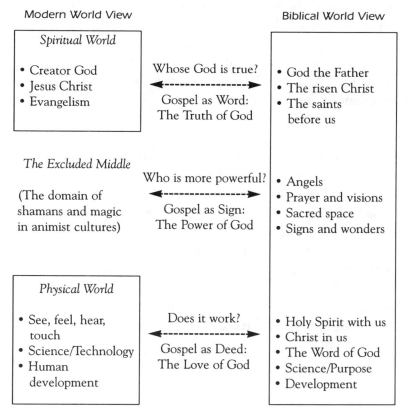

Modern World View   Biblical World View

Spiritual World		
• Creator God	Whose God is true?	• God the Father
• Jesus Christ	← - - - - - - - - →	• The risen Christ
• Evangelism	Gospel as Word: The Truth of God	• The saints before us

The Excluded Middle		
(The domain of shamans and magic in animist cultures)	Who is more powerful? ← - - - - - - - - → Gospel as Sign: The Power of God	• Angels • Prayer and visions • Sacred space • Signs and wonders

Physical World		
• See, feel, hear, touch	Does it work? ← - - - - - - - - →	• Holy Spirit with us
• Science/Technology	Gospel as Deed:	• Christ in us
• Human development	The Love of God	• The Word of God • Science/Purpose • Development

on). Different sorts of questions are appropriate to different levels. For instance, an upcoming airline flight prompts different questions, depending on the level at which a person asks the question (please refer to the three boxes under "Modern World View" in Figure 8.2 on page 129):

* *"Upper"*: Why does God allow disasters?
* *"Middle"*: Will my flight reach its destination without crashing?
* *"Lower"*: Under what conditions do airplanes crash?

While not arguing that we re-embrace the excluded middle—the reality of everything from leprechauns to zombies—Hiebert does observe that in some situations a pastor does better to exorcise than to demythologize, and that we should not be too quick to prefer the modern over the biblical world view. Regarding "word, deed and sign," the list reflects a recovery of the physical and "middle" worlds as areas that need to experience the gospel.

But in "The church ministering in word, deed and sign, recovering the whole," what is "recovering the whole" about? On the one hand, it signals that word, deed and sign do not represent—characteristically—three different areas of ministry coordinated by three different departments of the church. When folk from the Parish of the Resurrection or Ichthus canvas their neighborhoods asking, "how can we help you?" they may share Scripture, pray for healing, or help rebuild a roof, depending on the neighbor's response. So "the whole" has to do with the ministering body. On the other hand, it signals that our different dimensions are all interrelated, and that the addressing of any one of these dimensions must take integration into account.

B. Where is holism seen?

3. With the poor

> *The Lord works vindication*
>   *and justice for all who are oppressed.*
> *He made known his ways to Moses,*
>   *his acts to the people of Israel. (Ps. 103.6-7)*

Holistic mission characteristically happens among the poor (see points 5-6 in chapter seven). What does this mean? It does not mean that holistic mission happens only among the poor. It does mean that—as the ministry descriptions indicate—sooner or later the poor become part of the mission. It does mean that repeated decisions on the part of a church or mission not to include the poor raises the dangerous question of the applicability of Jesus' parable about Lazarus and the rich man. In this way, the poor provide a valuable reality check for most of the elements of holistic mission sketched in this chapter.

Let me present some observations.

Presently a wide variety of responses are given to the question of whether and how the ministering community should relocate into the community being ministered to. The variety of responses suggests that while a particular response may be right at one time and place for a particular group, the search for a universal response is probably misguided. (Scripture celebrates both Esther and Nehemiah as accomplishing God's purposes, Esther in the palace and Nehemiah in the rubble. What either of them might have made of this is another issue.)

As the ministry examples illustrate, work *among* the poor properly makes the transition to work *with* the poor. The poor, that is, increasingly define and respond to their own situation.

That holism involves the poor relates to Berkhof's analysis of the principalities and powers, since one of the fundamental claims the principalities and powers make is that only some of the members of a given society are necessary. The rest are redundant, or perhaps not even members. Where we encounter conversations about acceptable levels of unemployment or about which benefits "aliens" should or should not receive, we encounter conversations deeply shaped by the principalities and powers.

Who, by the way, are "the poor"? On the one hand, where the ministries described here focus on the poor, they focus on the materially poor. This is, I believe, the fundamental and the biblical starting point. On the other hand, because "poor" is subject to social definition and therefore the fickleness of the principalities and powers, any group can find themselves included.

C. How is holism expressed?

4. Through a rehearing of Scripture

This element appeared as "kingdom theology" in the previous chapter. I do not mean to devalue the kingdom by the shift in focus implied by "through a rehearing of Scripture," but to put its rediscovery in a larger context.

The Scripture has appeared in unformalized ways in a number of the cases. In John Bosco's experience, Proverbs 3:5-6 served as a turning point: "It suddenly occurred to John that if God was in this situation, then maybe he should try and help the workers" (Paul 1985, 5). Rick Thomas' ministry in El Paso, Texas (Our Lady's Youth Center), took a new turn as he shared Luke 14:12-14 (NIV) with a prayer group:

> Then Jesus said to his host, "When you give a luncheon or dinner, do not invite your friends, your brothers or relatives, or your rich neighbors; if you do, they may invite you back and so you will be repaid. But when you give a banquet, invite the poor, the crippled, the lame, the blind, and you will be blessed. Although they cannot repay you, you will be repaid at the resurrection of the righteous."

After praying about the meaning of this passage the members of the group decided that the passage was a call for them to reach out and care for the poor in a new way—to equip them as brothers and sisters in the Lord. They decided to cross the Rio Grande and share Christmas dinner with the poor who lived and worked in the *basurero* [garbage dump] of Juarez [Mexico] (Leavenworth 1988, 32).

These experiences parallel those connected with Scripture Search as practiced in World Vision's projects in the Philippines. As I described above, we find a profound shift going on from a reading which assumes that Scripture speaks to the individual about the soul in the world to come to a reading which assumes that Scripture speaks to the community about all dimensions of life in this world. (See further the findings report, Pentecostal and Charismatic and Evangelical Social Activist Conference, and the studies by Duncan and Robertson.)

5. Through an orientation of process over program

This corresponds to the "relational process" described in the previous chapter. As noted there, we can describe this element in two ways. First, we can describe it in terms of Hall's contrast between product-oriented and relational processes. Second, we can also describe this dimension as the contrast between meeting needs through the normal day-to-day life of the community, and meeting needs through specific programs.

This topic connects to the ongoing search for management tools appropriate for holistic mission (see, for instance, Escobar 1991). Within evangelical circles influenced by North America, the tools tend to be of the management-by-objective school, which has often represented an improvement. Nevertheless, management-by-objective is more obviously useful when we understand mission in terms of transferring goods (how many? by when?) or technology than when we understand it in terms of the empowerment of local communities. Whether we simply need to get better at writing subtler objectives or whether we need a different model is still an open question.

6. *Through a commitment to continual conversion or learning*

> For my thoughts are not your thoughts, neither are your ways my ways, says the Lord. For as the heavens are higher than the earth, so are my ways higher than your ways, and my thoughts than your thoughts. (Isa. 55.8-9)

This is a new element, implicit in at least some of the ministry descriptions. There are at least three issues here. They are, in order of increasing difficulty:

❖ The need for change to meet changing contexts (an organizational necessity);

❖ The need for the evangelist to change (and not just the evangelized); and

❖ The need to finally come to know the God of Jesus.

Regarding organizational necessity, one of the reasons groups like Ichthus and the Parish of the Resurrection appear in studies like this is that they are in touch with their context and have responded creatively to it. The challenge for these groups is to keep that affirmation in the present tense: to stay in touch with their context and to keep responding creatively to it. This is not easy, first because reading and creatively responding to a context is in itself an achievement. (Research cited by economist Lester Thurow suggests that in the business world people who have achieved instant wealth through capitalization do it only once: "The typical pattern is for a man to make a great fortune and then settle down and earn the market rate of return on his existing portfolio" [1980, 172-77]). Second, routinization (tradition) sets in very quickly. Third, groups that become known are celebrated (as in this book), increasing the temptation to say, "We've arrived!"

The second dimension of this commitment to continual conversion and learning is that of the change demanded of those who bring a message of change to others. Bartolomé de las Casas put the matter pointedly; one of his five essential elements for evangelization is that "the preaching be of benefit at least to the preachers" (1975, 241). Lesslie Newbigin develops the point by looking at the story of Peter and Cornelius in Acts 10:

> What the story makes clear, and what is spelled out in more theological terms (as we shall see) in the fourth Gospel, is that mission changes not only the world but also the church. Quite plainly in this case there is a conversion of the church as well as the conversion of Cornelius. It is not as though the church opened its gates to admit a new person into its company, and then closed them again, remaining unchanged except for the addition of a name to its roll of members. Mission is not just church extension. It is something more costly and more revolutionary. It is the action of the Holy Spirit who in his sovereign freedom both convicts the world (John 16:8-11) and leads the church toward the fullness of the truth which it has not yet grasped (John 16:12-15). Mission is not essentially an action by which the church puts forth its own power and wisdom to conquer the world around it; it is, rather, an action of God, putting forth the power of his Spirit to bring the universal work of Christ for the salvation of the world nearer to its completion. At the end of the story, which runs from Acts 10:1 to 11:18, the church itself became a kind of society different from what it was before Peter and Cornelius met. It had been a society enclosed within the cultural world of Israel: it became something radically different—a society which spanned the enormous gulf between Jew and pagan and was open to embrace all the nations which had been outside the covenant by which Israel lived. (Newbigin 1978, 66).

The need to finally come to know the God of Jesus is implicit in Newbigin's reading of Acts 10-11, for what is at stake is not only the nature of the church, but also of God. Segundo Galilea makes the point explicit:

> Let us not think, *a priori*, that a Christian believes in and prays to the Christian God: there are always ambiguities and idolatries in the God who is adored and followed. Knowledge of and conversion to the God of the Gospels is a lifelong task, for everyone. Spirituality ["the process of following Christ, under the direction of the Spirit, and beneath the guidance of the Church," p. 4] is the gradual conversion to the God of Jesus. (1988, 24)

One of the ways this third dimension has been working itself out in the World Vision Partnership has been through our work in encouraging the dignity of communities. Experience has shown that a critical part of the development of a community is an increase in self-respect and a willingness on the part of community to take itself, and its gifts, seriously. That is on the "development" side. On the "Christian" side, we have sometimes had to do an about-face, for some of us come from churches that tend to overlook or discourage human dignity (seeing it as a threat to God's dignity). In at least some cases the result has been that we have recovered an appreciation for the value God places on human dignity, a small—but not insignificant—shift in our image of God.

7. Through the local-global tension

This appeared in chapter seven as "world mission." Cross-cultural ministry in other parts of the world supplement and inform the group's local ministry. This serves both to check complacency (middle class groups in particular) and parochialism (all groups).

The phrase "local-global" recalls the slogan, "Think globally, act locally!" Recent contributions in the *International*

Review of Mission by Jan van Butselaar, general secretary of the Netherlands Missionary Council, and Kwame Bediako, founder director of the Akrofi-Kristaller Memorial Centre for Mission Research and Applied Theology (Ghana), help us to focus the issue.

Van Butselaar observes that "think globally, act locally" reflected the confidence in international ecumenical organizations:

> Conversion became a master-plan for (political or spiritual) change on a worldwide scale. Indications from Geneva (referring to the World Council of Churches), from Lausanne (referring to the Lausanne movement), or from other ecumenical bodies were to be followed. The assumption was that since these organizations operated on a universal level, they represented most fully the will of God for this world, and for the church worldwide. (1992, 367)

Reading the international gatherings at Manila (Lausanne in 1989) and Canberra (World Council of Churches in 1991) as evidence for the limitations of this model ("the ecumenical structures were not able to react adequately to the new momentum in world history"), van Butselaar suggests an inverted formula: "Thinking locally, acting—wherever needed—globally!" (1992, 372).

Bediako carries the reflection further. On the one hand, the church now has multiple geographic centers (reflecting the worldwide shifts in concentrations of Christians). On the other hand, every local Christian community has a "fundamentally ecumenical dimension" in that "Christianity itself, wherever it has emerged and continued . . . has done so by cross-cultural diffusion." Thus Bediako pictures the worldwide Christian community "as a series of overlapping circles, with peripheries touching centres, so that, in effect, every periphery is a potential centre, and vice versa" (1992, 376). Thus:

The nature of ecumenical relations is not between "small" and "local" contexts, on the one hand, and an "international" and "ecumenical" superstructure that directs or disciplines them, on the other; rather, it is that of the meeting and intersecting of the various "local" expressions and embodiments of faith in the Lord Jesus Christ, of all manifestations of mission in his name, as Jan van Butselaar rightly points out, "to exchange, to listen and to be listened to" (1992, 377).

8. Through small groups

And he appointed twelve, to be with him, and to be sent out to preach and have authority to cast out demons. (Mark 3.14-15)

This appeared in chapter seven as "small group" and "ministry groups." Starting from the vision of the mission itself, we have moved from the "where" to the "how," and now to the structural dimension of the "how." Small groups and leadership that serves the mission are the structural part of the "how."

It is in the small group that Scripture is heard and reheard. The small group births and nurtures the process-driven mission. (Some types of small groups are also the agent of mission.) The small group provides the context for continual conversion and learning. The small group provides the first anchor point of the local-global tension.

9. Through leadership that serves this mission

Whoever would be great among you must be your servant, and whoever would be first among you must be slave of all. For the Son of Man also came not to be served, but to serve, and to give his life as a ransom for many. (Mark 10:43b-45)

In the previous chapter, this issue appeared as "servant leadership" and "leadership training." While there is much truth to the saying, "The last thing to be converted is the pock-etbook," our use of power may be even more resistant to con-version.

A major piece of unfinished business is learning how to talk about this dimension and how to strengthen it. For this, some management literature looks promising. Robert K. Green-leaf's *Servant Leadership* is one point of reference. Another pos-sible point is Peter M. Senge's *Fifth Dimension*, in which he suggests:

> In essence, the leader's task is designing the learning processes whereby people throughout the organization can deal productively with the critical issues they face, and develop their mastery in the learning disciplines. (1990, 345)

If anything should have become clear in the last two chap-ters, it is that we are still learning what we can and should mean by "holistic ministry." Leadership that facilitates this continual learning is going to be essential. In a sense, all the points under "how" highlight some aspect of learning (and learning is obvi-ously not absent in "what" or "where").

NOTES

1   Thomas Merton, *Contemplation in a World of Action*, London: George Allen & Unwin Ltd., 1971, as cited by W. Paul Jones in "Hospitality within and without" [*Weavings* 9/1 (1994): 6-10], using inclusive language.

9

Finished and
Unfinished Business

What, then, is holistic ministry? As we noted in chapter one, "holistic" was first employed to describe an evange- lism ministry that also included attention to the "non-spiritual" needs of its audience. This continues to be the way most peo- ple use the word, although sometimes its use reflects a less dichotomized view of the world. Through a series of dialogues between evangelicals involved in social action and charismat- ics, "holistic" has been growing from "word and deed" to "word, deed and sign."

In MARC (Mission Advanced Research and Communica- tion, a division of World Vision International), we were in enough conversations in which "holistic" came up that we real- ized we needed more data. Also, World Vision's local teams wanted to reflect on the "holistic ministry" they continued to promote. So MARC began this study. To guide the study, we adopted this provisional definition of holism: "The Christian community is to be a sign of the kingdom, in which evangelism, social action, and the Spirit are present and inseparably related."

140

The table presented in chapter eight, reproduced as Figure 9.1 below, summarizes the results of this study.

If we ask the question, what does the holistic ministry that corresponds to this definition look like? the listing of elements in the left column indicates what we found. The first four elements (word, work and wonder; evangelism; social action; charismatic) are not surprising; they were built into the study's design.

The next two elements are option for the poor and incarnation. The first is probably not surprising, given that the study

Figure 9.1: Dimensions of holism in chapters 7-8

Chapter 7	Chapter 8
What is holism?	
1 Word, work and wonder 2 Evangelism 3 Social Action 4 Charismatic	1 The church as sign of the kingdom 2 The church ministering in word, deed and sign, recovering the whole
Where is holism seen?	
5 Option for the poor 6 Incarnation	3 With the poor
How is holism expressed?	
7 Kingdom theology 8 Relational process 9 World mission 10 Small group 11 Ministry groups 12 Leadership training 13 Servant leadership	4 Through a rehearing of Scripture 5 Through an orientation of process over program 6 Through a commitment to continual conversion and learning 7 Through the local-global tension 8 Through small groups 9 Through leadership that serves this mission

is being done from within World Vision. "Incarnation" is finally more a question than a theme: In what ways ought a group ministering with the poor share their life situation? This is hardly a new question. What is worthy of note and celebration is the number of ministries in which the poor themselves are ministering.

The surprise was what showed up in the "How is holism expressed?" section. The kingdom of God has moved from the seminary to the streets. It is not that long ago that books like John Bright's *The Kingdom of God* seemed somewhat esoteric. "Relational process" signals the arrival of the post-management-by-objective era. "World mission" is encouraging: intense local involvement is not breeding isolation, but sharing of resources. At the same time, world mission is not world-mission-as-usual, but world mission shaped by the practice of the other dimensions of holism. "Small group" (and "ministry groups") signals the need for a match between ministry and congregational structure. The ministries examined in this book suggest that holistic ministries drive and are driven by decentralization and personalization of congregational life. "Leadership training" as a priority among the ministries surveyed underscores the inadequacy of the status quo. "Servant leadership" signals the search for congruence between the ministry and the leadership given. If the ministry is about empowerment, the leadership needs to be empowering.

If the question is, what is the emerging shape of holistic mission that corresponds to this definition? the response is in the column on the right. There are two important shifts from the left to the right column.

First, "the church as sign of the kingdom" (the first element), highlights part of the definition and makes explicit what is implicit in the descriptions. Holistic ministry that brings good news to those "outside" is based on those "inside" experiencing this good news, not as passive recipients, "no longer strangers and sojourners, but . . . fellow citizens with the saints and members of the household of God, built upon the foundation of the apostles and prophets, Christ Jesus himself being the cornerstone, in whom the whole structure is joined together and grows into a holy temple in the Lord . . . a dwelling place of God in the Spirit" (Eph. 2:19-22).

The second shift is the inclusion of "through a commitment to continual conversion and learning." It is difficult to assess the strength of this element in the ministries reviewed. As described in the previous chapter, continual conversion and learning has a number of dimensions. On the one hand, it means staying in touch with one's context; ministries that fail here eventually become obsolete. On the other hand, it has to do with the link between ministry and spirituality.

This summary suggests two questions. First, is this list of elements complete? Second, what does the study imply?

Is this list of elements complete? No. Two elements were notable by their absence: family and vocation.

1. Family

One important effect of the Western cultural heritage has been taken up with a vengeance in the internationalizing marketplace. This effect is an individualism that leaves little space for the family, except as a focus for Dad's activity as consumer and provider of vacations or Mom's activity as consumer and provider of tasty meals and a spotless toilet. We can also see the spread of the value of individualism in holistic mission, in which characteristically the major foci for ministry are the individual, the community, or groups defined by need or proposed intervention. Much less often is the family perceived as a focal point for ministry. This practice of overlooking the family is less true, fortunately, to the degree that the ministry is incarnational and process-driven rather than program-driven. While there are ministries focusing on the family, these—at least in the United States—tend to be narrowly focused.

Articles by Vinay and Colleen Samuel (1993), Jorge E. Maldonado (1993) and the dissertation by Elizabeth Brusco (1986) call for more attention to the family. Brusco's dissertation, "The Household Basis of Evangelical Religion and the Reformation of Machismo in Colombia" is particularly interesting in this regard. Brusco argues:

> Within the confines of a strongly male dominated society such as Colombia, the revolutionary impact of evangelicalism is not that it transforms women's roles but that it has the power to change men to conform with female ideals and aspirations. (1986, 130)

In a survey of ministries to families, Maldonado notes that in the Brazilian *Comunidade Evangélica*, "North American authors such as Jaime Kemps (who lives in Brazil), Tim and Beverly Lahaye, Larry Christenson, James Dobson, and others were . . . frequently mentioned as influential" (1993, 224).

On the issue of family we are perhaps where we were in Pentecostal, charismatic and evangelical social activist relations not many years back. Clearly we need more research and coordinated attention to the matter of family.

2. Vocation

I recall a young Brazilian bank employee who was doing volunteer work with a poor community. As a volunteer he was helping to build a community center, and supporting one of the churches in the barrio. He was frustrated by the demands of his bank job, however, and was seriously considering resigning so that he would have more time to help the poor. It had not, apparently, crossed his mind that his bank job could be a means of serving the poor. Bank treatment of the poor, e.g., decisions on small-loan applications, affects whether people stay poor.

This bank employee is not unique. When we talk about holistic mission, the vast majority of Christians assume that we are not talking about their work, but about something for which they might volunteer their disposable time. The chief weakness of the collection of cases cited in this book is that they do not more substantially challenge this paradigm.

Ironically, the first of the *Transformation* studies (John Bosco in the factory in India) explores this direction—up to the point of John losing his job precisely because he understood it as the place to which God had called him. This is, of course, an inevitable risk, and the reason for proverbs such as "It is better to be of a lowly spirit with the poor than to divide the spoil with the proud" (Prov. 16:19). In other words, it would be easier to understand the contrasts between working *for, with* and *among* the poor if we were more often in the habit of performing those acts of obedience leading to sudden membership among the poor.

There are voices addressing the issue of vocation. Ray Bakke (International Urban Associates), Pete Hammond (Marketplace) and Frank Tilllapaugh (1982) are trying to communicate a vision of ministry in which one's work becomes one expression—if not the primary expression—of ministry. On the theological front, Miroslav Volf's *Work in the Spirit* provides tools for developing our reflection in this area.

What Does This Study Imply?

One implication of this study is the importance of process. For a variety of reasons, church or parachurch groups (or units within either) may be involved in selling a vision for holistic mission. This can be a service. At the same time, both the studies in general and Hall's distinction between product-oriented and relational processes suggest that growth in holistic mission reflects growth in the group as a whole—perhaps at more profound levels. Promotion of holistic mission as a package (a product) without careful attention to the internal processes of a group may be counter-productive.

For example, consider Duncan's historical summary (cited in chapter seven):

During the 1970s many churches in New Zealand experienced renewal and church growth. They came into new forms of worship, ministry and community. But after about a decade of inheriting one blessing after another some churches began to ask what it was all for. This question and an attempt to answer it really birthed Servants to Asia's Urban Poor.

How tempting it might have been to come in halfway through that decade with a prophetic call to holistic mission! Would we have gotten Servants to Asia's Urban Poor, or something else?

To summarize, taking process seriously means that the next step for a group is more likely to be suggested by its pilgrimage up to this point than by the latest monograph on holistic mission.

To put the point a different way, both the importance of process and the diversity of models should discourage the reduction of holism to a particular list of ingredients. Thus while this book's title, By Word, Work and Wonder captures an important moment in the evangelical conversation, we should not understand its lists as the answer to the question, what is holism?

A second implication of this study is the *missiological* significance of "the ordinariness of the church" (Hauerwas and Willimon). On the one hand, the presence of the ordinary (learning to forgive, to recognize an idol, and so on) is the presupposition for mission. On the other hand, what is striking about many of the ministries seen here is the appropriate fuzziness of the distinction between the ordinary and mission.

A third implication of this study is that the lists in Figure 9.1 may be of use in identifying how a group's ministry is being blocked. For instance, if a group is attempting to minister holistically while at the same time: (1) living from a theology in which the kingdom is absent; or (2) being organized internally solely in large groups; or (3) maintaining the leadership patterns "of the Gentiles," this study suggests that elements such as these may themselves be the points of blockage.

Other readers will see other implications, discern other gaps, produce more interesting lists. May the result be praise to the God who has been present in fresh and surprising ways in London, Bogota, Mexico City and Manila.

Bibliography

Abraham, William J. *The Logic of Evangelism*. Grand Rapids: Eerdmans, 1989.

Bediako, Kwame. "New paradigms on ecumenical cooperation: An African perspective." *International Review of Mission* 81 (1992): 375-79.

Berk, Stephen. 1989. "From proclamation to community: The Work of John Perkins." *Transformation* 6/4 (1989): 1-7.

Berkhof, Hendrikus. *Christ and the powers*. Herald Press, 1962.

Brusco, Elizabeth. "The Household basis of evangelical religion and the reformation of machismo in Columbia." Ph.D. diss., City University of New York, 1986.

CRESR [Consultation on the Relationship between Evangelism and Social Responsibility]. *Evangelism and social responsibility: An Evangelical commitment*. Lausanne Occasional Papers 21. Lausanne Committee for World Evangelization, 1982.

Casas, Bartolomé de las. *Del unico modo de atraer a todos los pueblos a la verdadera religión*. Colección Popular 137. Mexico: Fondo de Cultura Económica, 1537.

Dayton, Donald W. *Discovering an Evangelical Heritage*. Hendrickson, 1976.

Duncan, Michael. "A Journey in the slums of Asia." *Transformation* 10/3 (1993): 23-26.

Escobar, Samuel. "Missiology in the Lausanne movement." *Transformation* 8/4 (1991): 7-13.

Forster, Roger. "Ichthus Christian Fellowship," in *Ten New Churches*, edited by R. Forster, London: MARC Europe, 1986.

Forster, Roger. "Ichthus Christian Fellowship, London." *Transformation* 9/2 (1992): 15-18, 23.

Galilea, Segundo. *The Way of Living Faith: A Spirituality of Liberation*. San Francisco: Harper & Row, 1988.

Gitari, Grace. "Evangelical development in Mount Kenya East." *Transformation* 5/4 (October/December 1988): 44-46.

Greenleaf, Robert K. *Servant Leadership*. Mahwah, New Jersey: Paulist Press, 1977.

Grigg, Viv. *Companion to the Poor: Christ in the Urban Slums*. Rev. ed. Monrovia, Calif.: MARC, 1990.

Hall, Douglas. "A View from Boston's inner city." *Transformation* 9/2 (1992): 19-23.

Hathaway, Brian. "The Spirit and Social Action—A Model." *Transformation* 5/4 (1988): 40-43.

Hauerwas, Stanley and William Willimon. *Resident Aliens: Life in the Christian Colony*. Nashville: Abingdon, 1989.

Hauerwas, Stanley & William Willimon. "Why resident aliens struck a chord." *Missiology* 19/4 (1991): 419-29.

Hiebert, Paul. "Spiritual warfare: Biblical perspectives." *Mission Focus* 20/3 (1992): 41-46.

Klaus, Ronald L. "Social action and the concept of 'Immanuel': The experience of the Living Word Community, Philadelphia." *Transformation* 5/4 (1988): 34-40.

Leavenworth, Paul G. "Good news for the poor: A Case study of the ministry of Father Rick Thomas." *Transformation* 5/4 (October/December 1988): 32-33.

Lohfink, Gerhard. *Jesus and Community: The Social Dimension of Christian Faith*. Minneapolis: Fortress Press, 1984.

Maldonado, Jorge E. "Evangelicalism and the family in Latin America." *International Review of Mission* 82 (1993): 189-202.

Marsden, George M. *Fundamentalism and American Culture: The Shaping of Twentieth-Century Evangelicalism 1870-1925*. New York: Oxford University Press, 1980.

McAlpine, Thomas H. "La Parroquia de la Resurrección, Mexico City." *Transformation* 10/2 (1993): 28-32.

Mitchell, Roger. *The Kingdom Factor: An Introduction to Living in the Kingdom of God*. San Francisco: Marshall Pickering, 1986.

Neighbour, Ralph W., Jr. *Where Do We Go from Here? A Guidebook for the Cell Group Church*. Houston: Touch, 1990.

Newbigin, Lesslie. *The Open Secret: Sketches for a Missionary Theology*. Grand Rapids: Eerdmans, 1978.

Newbigin, Lesslie. 1989. *The Gospel in a Pluralist Society*. Grand Rapids: Eerdmans, 1989.

Padilla, C. René. "How evangelicals endorsed social responsibility 1966-1983." *Transformation* 2/3 (1985): 27-33.

Paul, Robin. "The Spirit and justice: A model for reflection and action." *Transformation* 2/2 (1985): 5-8.

Pentecostal/Charismatic and Evangelical Social Activist Conference, Sierra Madre 1988. "Findings Report." *Transformation* 5/4 (1988):1-2.

Robertson, Murray. "Renewal brings new life." *Transformation* 8/4 (1991): 19-22.

Samuel, Vinay and Colleen. "Rebuilding families: A Priority for wholistic mission." *Transformation* 10/3 (1993): 5-7.

Sanchez, Sergio. "Personal pilgrimage to the development of the Mexican Association for Rural and Urban Transformation (AMEXTRA, A.C.)." *Transformation* 10/3 (1993): 13-16.

Scott, Waldron. "The Paterson paradigm: Some personal reflections." *Transformation* 8/4 (1991): 16-18,22.

Senge, Peter M. *The Fifth Discipline: The Art and Practice of the Learning Organization*. New York: Doubleday, 1990.

Stuart, Morris. "Building the Kingdom in sunburnt soil." *Transformation* 3/3 (1986): 17-22.

Thurow, Lester C. *The Zero-Sum Society*. New York: Basic Books, 1980.

Tillapaugh, Frank R. *The Church Unleashed: Getting God's People Out Where the Needs Are*. Ventura, Calif.: Gospel Light, 1982.

van Butselaar, Jan. "Thinking locally, acting globally: The Ecumenical movement in the new era." *International Review of Mission* 81/323 (1992): 363-373.

Volf, Miroslav. *Work in the Spirit: Toward a Theology of Work.* New York: Oxford University Press, 1991.